BILL BRIGHT   RON JENSON

GLOW

IN THE DARK

Multnomah® Publishers *Sisters, Oregon*

GLOW IN THE DARK
published by Multnomah Publishers, Inc.

© 2005 by Ron Jenson and Bright Media Foundation
International Standard Book Number: 1-59052-485-3

Cover image by Lauren Krohn/Photonica

Unless otherwise indicated, Scripture quotations are from:
New American Standard Bible® © 1960, 1977, 1995
by the Lockman Foundation. Used by permission.
Other Scripture quotations are from:
The Holy Bible, New International Version (NIV)
© 1973, 1984 by International Bible Society,
used by permission of Zondervan Publishing House
Holy Bible, New Living Translation (NLT)
© 1996. Used by permission of Tyndale House Publishers, Inc.
All rights reserved.
The Holy Bible, New King James Version (NKJV)
© 1984 by Thomas Nelson, Inc.
The Holy Bible, King James Version (KJV)

Multnomah is a trademark of Multnomah Publishers, Inc.,
and is registered in the U.S. Patent and Trademark Office.
The colophon is a trademark of Multnomah Publishers, Inc.

Printed in the United States of America

ALL RIGHTS RESERVED
No part of this publication may be reproduced, stored in a retrieval system,
or transmitted, in any form or by any means—electronic, mechanical,
photocopying, recording, or otherwise—without prior written permission.

For information:
MULTNOMAH PUBLISHERS, INC. • 601 N. LARCH ST. • SISTERS, OR 97759

Library of Congress Cataloging-in-Publication Data
Bright, Bill.
  Glow in the dark / Bill Bright and Ron Jenson.
      p. cm.
  Includes bibliographical references.
  ISBN 1-59052-485-3
  1.   Christian life.   I. Jenson, Ron. II. Title.
  BV4501.3.B7524 2005
  248.4—dc22

                                      2005004361

05 06 07 08 09 10—10 9 8 7 6 5 4 3 2 1 0

"Each one of us as responsible Christians asks, 'How can I make a difference for righteousness in our present-day culture? What can we do to be redemptive instruments in God's kingdom?' This valuable book provides insight, guidance, and direction in answering these pervasive questions. I commend it without hesitation. Both authors have been longtime friends of mine and are, by their experience, highly qualified to bring this kind of light to a darkened society."

TED W. ENGSTROM, PRESIDENT EMERITUS, WORLD VISION

"Dr. Bill Bright always lived up to his last name. He was a brilliant beacon of God's amazing grace to a lost and confused world. He shined *brightly* up until the moment he took his last breath. Now, teamed with one of his most cherished understudies, we all can learn the *why* and the *how* of being torchbearers of God's love. Bright and Jenson will teach you how to increase your spiritual wattage as well as direct the beam of your light as you make yourself more available to God to glow in the dark."

DR. TIM KIMMEL, AUTHOR OF *LITTLE HOUSE ON THE FREEWAY*
AND *GRACE-BASED PARENTING*

"Bill's life not only influenced me, but countless others throughout the world to love God more deeply and shine His light broadly. Hallmarks of Bill's life were a Holy Spirit–filled life, a heart to see the world reached for Christ, and never losing his first love. Ron Jenson has pioneered demonstrating Bill's desire to make Christ known to men and women leading in challenging parts of our culture."

DR. STEVE DOUGLASS
PRESIDENT, CAMPUS CRUSADE FOR CHRIST, INT'L

"At a time when the effects of post-modernism pose a challenge to Christians everywhere, *Glow in the Dark* helps in the transformation of our reductionistic understanding of salvation to a mature Christian walk and an outstanding personal and global witness for Christ. *Glow in the Dark* is a must-read for every Christian."

DR. APPIANDA ARTHUR, DIRECTOR OF CHURCH RELATIONS, INTERNATIONAL JUSTICE MISSION

"Want a more effective life? *Glow in the Dark* will help you maximize every area of your life—at home, work, church, and in your community. I'd suggest you buy two copies—one for you and another for your pastor."

DENNIS RAINEY, PRESIDENT, FAMILYLIFE

"The contents are just as impactful as the title."

BOB SAFFORD, PRIMERICA FINANCIAL SERVICES, FIRST INTERNATIONAL SALES DIRECTOR, LONDON, ENGLAND

"'Is it really possible to have joy in all circumstances? How do I know God's will for my life, or even just for today? Why are my friendships with other men often superficial?' This book addresses these great questions and many others. Ron Jenson is a master at bringing biblical truth to life in a way that will increase your faith, touch your heart, and change your behavior."

KEVIN JENKINS, MANAGING DIRECTOR, TRIWEST CAPITAL PARTNERS, CALGARY, CANADA
FORMER PRESIDENT, CANADIAN AIRLINES

ACKNOWLEDGMENTS

On behalf of both of us, we would like to thank our wives, Vonette Bright and Mary Jenson, for co-laboring with us in life and ministry all these years.

Thank you to Matt Jenson (Ron's son) and Mary Jenson, for their hours of contribution to the content and format of this book. You are bright lights out there.

We are very grateful for the hard work and editorial advice from our literary representative, Janet K. Grant.

And thank you, Helmut Teichert, chief operating officer of the Bright Media Foundation, for working with us on behalf of the Bright family.

And I (Ron) want to thank you, Bill, for teaching me how to glow in the dark as a college student and encouraging, supporting, and believing in me through your words, actions, and stunning model of faith.

CONTENTS

Can't You Just Picture It?

▶▶What do you think of when you hear the name *Nobel*?

Most people think of the Nobel Peace Prize. Of course! The very mention of the name brings thoughts of world peace and honoring the planet's outstanding peacemakers. Think about the profound, ongoing impact of that coveted award!

But it wasn't always that way. Not at all. In fact, that name association wouldn't come until later in the life of Alfred Nobel. For most of his life, he was known for something very, very different.

At the height of Alfred's business success, his older brother died. By mistake a French newspaper printed Alfred's obituary instead of his brother's. In essence, the article read, "Alfred Nobel passed away yesterday. He made his millions by creating weapons of mass destruction for the annihilation of mankind."

It was only too true. Nobel invented, manufactured, and distributed dynamite and other explosives, sending his products all over the world. He had made his money exactly as the newspaper reported.

Seeing this in print, however, was like a slap in the face for Alfred. *Was that to be his legacy? Was that how history would remember him?* It was a wake-up call to reassess his life and impact…and to begin building a lasting legacy quite different from the one portrayed in his premature obituary.

We know the rest of his story. He took his money, time, and skills and spent the rest of his life investing in peace. And that's how we remember him. Instead of recalling the death, destruction, and mayhem created by his explosives, we think about a high and lofty prize promoting peace in a troubled world.

Alfred Nobel had the opportunity to read his own obituary—while he was still alive. But that won't happen for most of us. If we're going to gain any kind of perspective on the impact of our lives, it will mean taking time for some thinking and assessment. Have you done that? Have you ever wondered if your life is really making a difference? Do you have a sense of destiny—that you were created to leave a positive and powerful legacy?

As young men we both had plans for our lives based on what we thought would serve us well in the future. We had no need of God, we thought, and it seemed life was very much about materialism—wealth, houses, cars, travel, fame. But when we came up against the compelling and exciting person of Jesus Christ, everything changed.

Everything.

From that moment on, we knew we could never be happy, fulfilled, or ultimately secure living in light of such shortsighted plans. At different times and through different circumstances we presented ourselves to Christ—all we were and all we had—opening our minds to His agenda.

And we've never looked back.

Neither of us has ever entertained longing thoughts about what "might have been." Not a day has gone by that we haven't thanked Him for transforming us from the inside out and then giving us the most meaningful work a human being could ever imagine.

That's why this book you now hold in your hands is so important to us.

We chose the title, *Glow in the Dark: A Life That Lights the Way,* for at least two reasons.

First, *glow* underlines God's call for us to be His light, shining on a hill.

Second, we are to glow *in the dark.* We live in desperately needy times, with fingers of darkness penetrating our culture, our neighborhoods, our homes, and even ourselves. Though we are "new creatures in Christ," we must deal with our own sin, baggage, and bad habits on a daily basis—just as we are confronted with the sin, baggage, and bad habits of others.

So we choose to focus on the Light of the World to glow through our own darkness and that of the world at large. God's Word assures us that "those who look to him are radiant; their faces are never covered with shame" (Psalm 34:5, NIV).

Night falls rapidly across our culture. And yes, there's a real battle out there, with real casualties. But it's still possible to find our place in God's plan for lighting the way in that darkness. It's still possible to create *a legacy of light and life* beyond what you've ever imagined. To do so, we must acknowledge two warring kingdoms in the spiritual realm—Satan's kingdom of darkness and bondage and God's kingdom of light and freedom. Darkness and light cannot coexist. When one enters the scene, the other departs. God's design is that the darkness would be banished as His kingdom of light expands—and His plan involves us as His frontline, light-bearing soldiers.

A. W. Tozer put it well when he contrasted the attitude of early Americans with that of those in the twentieth (and twenty-first) century:

In the early days, when Christianity exercised a dominant influence over American thinking, men conceived the world to be a battleground. Our fathers believed in sin and the devil and hell as constituting one force; and they believed in God and righteousness and heaven as the other.... Man, so our fathers held, had to choose sides; he could not be neutral. For him it must be life or death, heaven or hell, and if he chose to come out on God's side he could expect open war with God's enemies. The fight would be real and deadly and would last as long as life continued here below.... The Christian soldier...never forgot what kind of world he lived in. It was a battleground, and many were the wounded and the slain.[1]

Tozer goes on to the modern mind-set, which certainly applies to us today:

How different today: the fact remains the same but the interpretation has changed completely. Men think of the world, not as a battleground but as a playground. We are not here to fight, we are here to frolic. We are not in a foreign land, we are at home. We are not getting ready to live, we are already living, and the best we can do is to rid ourselves of our inhibitions and our frustrations and live this life to the full.[2]

Tozer was right to remind us that the world is a battleground. If we're not even aware of the war, we may find ourselves in danger of committing treason.

Treason? Yes, and here's the definition: "Violation of allegiance toward one's sovereign or country; especially, the betrayal of one's own country by waging war against it or by consciously and purposely acting to aid its enemies."

Now, most Christians would never consciously commit treason against God's kingdom; they wouldn't think of it. But some are helping the enemy just the same by refusing to acknowledge the war. Under the cloak of their indifference, Satan is allowed to pursue his destructive operations unchallenged.

Challenged or not, the battle is a firefight on every front. And it's time we join the ranks, shake off our lethargy, push through our uncertainty, and set aside our fears. It's not going away, this war, and while it is both defensive (battling with our own sin, Satan, and the world system) and offensive (positively and winsomely impacting the culture on an ongoing and intentional basis), the outcome has already been decided. And we are the victors!

We will begin our book by addressing the nature of this war and its most important and most vulnerable front—the mind.

Next, we will look briefly at some of the challenges in our society and how each of us can make a difference.

Finally, the balance of the book will deal with solutions. We are big believers in *glancing* at the problems (thinking critically) and *gazing* at the solutions (having a positive, can-do spirit).

Be prepared for a forthright, hands-on overview of the battle before us. Along the way, we'll provide real-life examples of how to experience life at its best—even though the war rages around us. We believe that healthy, right-living individuals with biblically centered minds build healthy, intact families. These families gather to form the body of Christ in healthy, proactive churches. Such churches ensure healthy, productive, upright institutions, which shape strong, vibrant societies.

Change—and ultimate victory—is a process that moves from the inside out. Can't you picture a day when a growing number of people in the world live in peace and joy because they've been trained to think, love, work, and relate by the Word of God? Can't you picture, on some future day, strong economies based on truth and integrity, strong race relations based on a biblical understanding of the value and dignity of all human life, strong churches unified around the person of Christ, and strong families with servant hearts and actions to back them up?

We can.

It's what makes us pound the table with excitement. It's what gets us up in the morning.

More than that, it's what we all were made for.

1

Learning to See in the Dark

Thinking Biblically

▶▶ *On February 20, without even realizing it, Hallie stepped into a fierce, ongoing war.*

She awoke tired but smiling with the vague recollection of her dream—a cute guy, a horse, and some kind of springtime scene with rolling hills she couldn't quite identify. Trying to recapture the dream, she had stayed under covers just a little bit too long...and now she would really have to scramble to make the train.

Still...it was nice waking in the dead of winter with spring in your mind.

She rushed through her shower and stood before her closet wondering what to put on. What do you wear to a job interview when you've never been there and don't know how they dress? Was this "casual Friday" or not? What kind of impression would she make? A wave of panic clutched at her, but she pushed it away. No time for that. She pulled out a dark brown suit with a short skirt—not too short, but enough to show off her legs. It wouldn't hurt to use every advantage she had.

As her protein shake whirred in the blender, she glanced through the devotional for the day, praying even as she read that God would forgive her for giving her morning to her dream guy and not to Him. On the refrigerator she had taped a Bible verse she wanted to memorize. Yet it had been there so long she rarely saw it anymore—and had to relearn it nearly every time it caught her eye. This morning, on her way out the door, she peeled it off the fridge and tucked it into her coat pocket.

After her dream about a warm spring day and Prince Charming, the blast of cold air took her breath and her smile away. She didn't have far to walk to the train, but every step was treacherous with the threat of black ice. Her coat whipped open if she didn't turn a little to the side, and by the time she entered the small station she had a crick in her neck and a scowl on her face. Spring seemed a lifetime away.

Waiting for the train, Hallie had a take-stock moment: a twenty-eight-year-old single woman in Berwyn, Pennsylvania, whose best friend was her mother in Cincinnati; a dead-end job selling advertising; no boyfriends. Except in her dreams. She wasn't unhappy exactly, but growing more unsettled about her *life. This was not what she had planned.*

The train was nearly full when it got to Hallie's stop. She hated walking down the aisle of a full train with all eyes upon her. Surely they were noticing the tiny moth hole on her coat, that she hadn't plucked her eyebrows recently, that her hair was a little too long, that her shoes and purse didn't match. A little light flickered and faded from her eyes, but she didn't notice it.

She opened her newspaper to the front page, intending to get lost in an engrossing national/international news story about Iraq or politics, but the sexual exploits of certain Hollywood and sports figures stole the headlines. The business section chided her for not having a stock portfolio; the health and food section convinced her she could lose ten pounds if she'd walk ten thousand steps a day; the lifestyle section told her brown was NOT the color this year; the entertainment section showed her one more time that she couldn't measure up in the "curb appeal" department.

Hallie discarded her paper behind her on an empty seat and turned to stare out the window. Collecting heavily upon her slumping shoulders were all the little, niggling feelings of inadequacy and indecision that she wrestled with so often. She gazed glassy-eyed at the buildings the train was rattling past. She had left her apartment hopeful and smiling, but now she could feel her optimism melting away like the ice tracked in on the floor of the train. Her Bible verse lay deep and untouched in her pocket.

The battle for Hallie's mind was hot and intense as the train rumbled toward downtown Philadelphia, and she was ready to wave the white flag.

Warfare and Worldview

We are at war! Make no mistake. The terrain may be unfamiliar. The terminology may be different. The tools may be surprising. The target may at times be difficult to define. But we are at war—and this is the greatest of wars.

It is a war of kingdoms.

Light versus darkness.

And the battleground is our minds.

In retrospect, most of us can point to moments in our daily lives where the battle for our minds and attitudes seems clearly defined. On the freeway in heavy traffic, in conversations with family members (no matter how well we get along), flipping through the myriad TV channels in the privacy of our homes.

Like Hallie, we also do battle without even knowing it, and often those are the skirmishes we lose. It's pretty easy to recognize warfare when you're talking about a rude cashier or an aggressive driver who cuts you off in traffic. But then there are those times when Satan drops a single thought into your mind. *I'll never be good enough.* Unless you've stocked your arsenal with *true* statements from God's Book of Truth, you'll be quickly overwhelmed, with little hope of overcoming.

Every day of our lives we live through microwars, seen and unseen, recognizable and unrecognizable. Some we lose, and some we win. And if we do come out on top, chances are it's because we've learned how to identify and deal with the enemy on this level.

There's a lot to be said for that—identifying and dealing with the enemy. The unknown is a much more terrifying proposition than the known. Knowledge, in this sense, *is* power. Bible knowledge accompanied by faith and the Holy Spirit means victory.

Our one sure hope is that this daily war for our minds is already won! Jesus' triumph over sin, death, and the devil, and His promise to return and re-create the heavens and the earth are a breathtakingly hopeful, joyful backdrop against which to do battle.

Yet, we *are* at war. This simple, profound admission is the first step in learning to see in the dark. It's the clicking on of the flashlight that will help you discern your path. Or better yet, it's the donning of a pair of night-vision goggles that will allow you to pick your way through the darkness, and prepare for what lies ahead.

Let's look a little more in depth at the contours of this war. Let's find out whether we're serving as faithful soldiers or unwittingly aiding and abetting the enemy.

Strategic Warfare

It's a long way from the days of World War II to today's War on Terror. The rules of conventional warfare have gone out the window. The sheer size of armies and the raw power of armaments no longer guarantee victory. Instead of division after division of ground troops, we now think in terms of "cells," "fringe groups," mass media campaigns, and strategic communications.

Power has given way to placement.

Brute strength to subtle analysis.

This dramatic shift in warfare has been crowned by the stunning success of a relatively small, underground movement of pockets of individuals. These new-era fighters have altered the contours and course of the world, using cataclysmic events (9/11) to be sure—but just as much attacking the minds and hearts of people.

The spiritual battle between the kingdoms of light and darkness is closely related, focusing as it does on the minds and worldviews of men and women. We, as Christians, must recapture the initiative and strategy in winning hearts and minds.

But there is a difference.

Rather than *imposing* a human viewpoint, we seek to expose people to the mind and will, the beauty and majesty, of Jesus Christ. Our job is to present a biblical view of the world and life which is compelling, morally appealing, and offers a positive hope for the future, for the individual, and for society.

This is not a "bodies and bullets" approach that seeks to subdue an enemy by sheer size and strength. Rather than beating back the darkness, it's more like piercing the darkness with laser beams, illuminating individual lives. While we are to overpower Satan and the powers of darkness, we are also to work toward the *transformation* of the people and systems that are subject to them.

Ours is a delicate business. We've been called to persuade rather than coerce, to transform rather than destroy. This calls for our own version of special operations warfare. And Objective Number One is *to win the minds of men and women.*

A Clash of Worldviews

Look at these common phrases that reflect what many believe across the world today:

"Everything is relative."

"You can do anything you want, as long as it doesn't hurt anybody."

"Just use common sense."

"You can't legislate morality."

"It may be right for you, but it's not right for me."

"Don't be so narrow-minded."

"How could it be wrong when it feels so right?"

"Look out for number one."

Many Christians accept the worldviews represented by these phrases without biblical evaluation. They have been, as J. B. Phillips's translation puts it, squeezed into the world's mold (Romans 12:2). Satan wants us to think that phrases like the ones above are harmless. But as we see them, hear them, and ultimately use them, the underlying assumptions subtly become ours, clouding our spiritual vitality and impact.

What is a Worldview?

A few years ago while flying across the country, I (Ron) had a fascinating discussion with a very sharp lawyer. A graduate of Harvard Law School, she was thirty-something, bright, and engaging.

She asked me what I did. I told her I was a coach.

"What kind of coach?" she asked.

"A life coach."

"Really? What does a life coach do?"

"It's my job to help people make their lives work."

Her reply was frank and immediate. "Well, I need that. I need help."

Then she asked me what I taught, and I began going through the ten core principles I use to help people deal with stress, resolve conflict, gain life balance, and build good habits. Each time I explained one she said she needed help in that area.

"What's the most important principle?" she finally asked.

All of them, I explained, were vital and universally applicable. But the taproot principle was to energize internally by building your character and your inner spiritual life.

"I don't have any spiritual life," she said.

"Oh yes," I said, "you do."

We went back and forth on this for a while, her denying any spirituality and my insisting on it. In fact, I told her that she had god (with a small g) at the center of her life.

"You can't say that!" she told me, a little heated. "You can't say I have God as the center of my life! I'm an atheist and don't even believe in God!"

"Yes, you do—and I can prove it."

"How?"

"Let me first define my terms. I'm calling your 'god' whatever is in control of your life. It's your boss, your power source, the thing that drives you. So when I say we all have god at the center of our life, that's what I'm getting at. For some people, that might be money. For others, it might be power or family or work or sex. What is it for you?"

"I don't know," the woman replied.

"Well then, I guess that must mean you're your own god," I said. "And—pardon me for asking—doesn't that make you a little nervous? I wouldn't want you to be *my* god. Now don't get me wrong. You seem like a great person. Probably a better person than I am. But I'm sure I wouldn't want to be *my* own god. That's way too big of a responsibility, and I know I'd screw it up every time...."

From there we went on to have a rich conversation about spiritual things. Whether she recognized it or not, I was beginning a process of discipleship with this woman. And even though I doubt I'll ever see her again, I believe that by pointing out her worldview and sharing mine, I helped open a door for her to think about her life in a new way.

A worldview is a mental blueprint or map, an organizing grid or model used to interpret and explain reality and to guide in moral decisions. Everyone has a worldview, whether or not he or she is aware of it, or whether or not it is highly developed. And our worldview is encouraged or discouraged, changed, and tweaked, at just about every point of our day. Many factors contribute to our worldview, including where and when we were born, peer pressure, our parents, our education, mass media, the Bible (or lack of it), the church, and other forces.

Did you watch Saturday morning cartoons as a child? For many of us, Bugs Bunny, the Road Runner, and Yogi Bear helped shape the way we think, make decisions, and live our lives. What cartoons help paint the background of your mind? The cartoons we remember always had good guys and bad guys—and the bad guys are always 100 percent bad, and the good guys are 100 percent good. The good guys always win, of course. But we also saw that maybe violence is an okay thing if it stops the bad guys. What influence might these lessons have on one's approach to crime? Or immigration? Or international relations? Or what we think of ourselves when we sin?

Our worldview is both dynamic and static. It is dynamic in that it is continually being formulated, but it is static in that we constantly use it to explain our existence, to give order to the world in which we live, and to guide our decisions. Our worldview either consciously or unconsciously shapes our ideas, thoughts, attitudes, beliefs, and values. The challenge we face is to acquire a worldview that adequately answers basic questions such as: What is real? Who is man? What is the basis of morality? What is the meaning of human history?

Adopting a Biblical Worldview

So what do worldviews have to do with glowing in the dark?

Just this: Until we make the choice to live with a biblical worldview, we *can't* glow in the dark. We won't be bright enough to penetrate the darkness. To have a transforming impact in any culture, we must be transformed ourselves. Romans 12:2 tells us that we are transformed "by the renewing of our mind." So, in putting on the mind of Christ, in developing a biblical worldview, we begin the process of both setting up a guard around our lives and penetrating the darkness with light.

I (Ron) was a little hoodlum as a preteen. What do you say about a kid who almost flunked kindergarten because he got in so many fights? In elementary school I was a consistent D- student. My fourth-grade report card from Mr. Kono had a sad consistency about it: straight D's except for one D- and one C-. But in the column marking "Effort," I had straight E's for excellent, the best you could get. Imagine what that said to me: "Ronnie's stupid, but he's maximizing his potential!"

If schoolwork was an uphill journey, my social life was Mount Everest. My nickname as a kid was Jelly-Belly Jenson, because I was so overweight. At ten years old I weighed twenty pounds too much to play peewee football! Then, maybe because I was so eager to belong, I developed some very destructive friendships. We began to dabble with forgery, but even worse, we set up a little pornography shop in my basement.

When I was thirteen, I was invited to a church camp where I heard the truth about God and what He thinks about me. When the camp speaker gave an invitation to receive Jesus, I thought, what do I have to lose? Absolutely nothing.

So I took the step to become a follower of Christ that weekend. In God's kind providence, I was paired up right away with a godly man who spent regular time with me for several months. Every time we'd meet he'd find something to say to me to encourage me. (And some days must have been a chore!) He'd say, "Ronnie, you talk a lot. Now, what you're saying isn't all that hot, but someday you just might be a speaker." Or, "Ronnie, kids follow you. Now, son, you're not always going in the right direction, but one day I bet you'll be a real leader."

This man, like no other, taught me that I had choices about how I lived my life. He revolutionized the way I thought of myself, and because of the transformation of my thinking, I was motivated to change. In just months I lost a lot of weight, and pushed my grades up from D's to A's— where they stayed through the rest of my schooling. I moved up the social scale from troublemaker to class president, and eventually to student body president in high school.

I wasn't smarter, more athletic, or better looking! What had changed?

My worldview.

I now had a beginning understanding of the character of God—and a new appreciation for how He saw me. And that meant everything.

Learning the character of God is the first set of truths to "put on" as we formulate our biblical worldview. We start here, learning all we can of who God is, what He's like, how He operates, what He thinks. We don't dabble in the Bible to find this out, we feast in it. We dedicate a portion of each day to discovering what God says about Himself. It's that simple.

Many years ago, I (Bill) was interviewed by Dr. James Boice on a radio program called *The Bible Hour*. One of the first questions he asked me was, "What is the most important truth to teach believers?" That sat me back in my chair for a moment. No one had ever asked me that question, and I was totally unprepared for it. I am convinced the Holy Spirit gave me the answer—even though I was a little surprised by my own reply.

"The attributes of God," I said.

I've had many years now to think about that question, and I'm more convinced now than ever that there is nothing more important to teach believers than what our God is really like. I've made it my focus in recent years to encourage people to study God's attributes.[3]

Why? Because our view of God determines our lifestyle. What we believe to be true about God's nature and character affects our work and leisure, the friends we choose, the type of literature we read, our sense of community and nation, our view of the world, and even the music we listen to.

Life won't make sense until God does.

The next truth we must examine as we form a biblical worldview is the truth about us. You might think we would begin at that point. But we can't. The fact is, what we think about ourselves might be miles from reality. Instead, we draw our reality from God's eternal word. We delve into the Bible to find out God's perspective about these creatures He fashioned after His own likeness (Genesis 1:26–31).

And what do we discover?

- That we are chosen, loved, formed, and given a purpose (Psalm 139:13–14; Genesis 1:28; Ephesians 1).
- That God has planned our days, disciplines us with love, and hopes for an intimate relationship with every one of us (Psalm 139:16; Jeremiah 29:11; Revelation 3:20).
- That we are inclined to turn away from God, and walk in ways that ultimately lead to our destruction (Isaiah 65:2; Romans 3:23; 6:23).

Along the way we discover God's hope for the world, how to deal with others, and how to develop our dependency upon Him. And we meet a recurring and troublesome character, Satan, who's out to destroy the whole plan, and to rob each of us of peace, purpose, and freedom.

Satan may not sound like much of a threat. Many who call themselves Christians have trouble imagining such a being. And when they do, he looks like he just stepped out of a cartoon (there's that cartoon again), a horned, mischievous, skinny, red guy with a slightly intriguing glint in his eye. In reality he is one of the most beautiful beings God ever created. His original name was Lucifer—Son of the Morning—and God placed him over all the heavenly hosts. But Lucifer was not content with his position, and he determined to become like God Himself. He led a revolt and took one third of the angels with him. That revolt continues today, though it is hopeless, for God has made all the provisions for total victory.

Satan's most effective tool is inserting a small lie within a large truth. "Yes, you are God's child…but you don't deserve His love and attention." Or, "Yes, God is trustworthy to provide for you…but you haven't asked Him the right way." Or, "Yes, the marriage bed is sacred…but you married the wrong woman."

According to preacher and theologian Donald Barnhouse, Satan's objective in the battle of the Garden of Eden was twofold: "He wished to detach man from God, and to attach man to himself. Man is dependent upon God and if that dependence is destroyed, something must take its place; the devil hoped that it would be a dependence upon himself."[4] Satan's objectives are the same today.

Understanding these cosmic schemes is the foundation of a biblical worldview, and further clarifies the nature of the warfare that shakes the world around us. Eventually, we all must acknowledge that we are either God's friends or His enemies, either living in the kingdom of light or the kingdom of darkness. There is no option for neutrality or indifference. And, contrary to John Lennon's hit song from a couple decades ago, you can't just imagine it all away.

Strategic Thinking

German pastor Martin Niemoeller painted a stark picture of another side of Germany during the rise of Hitler and the subsequent holocaust in which more than 11 million people were exterminated:

> In Germany they first came for the Communists and I didn't speak up because I wasn't a Communist.
>
> Then they came for the Jews, and I didn't speak up because I wasn't a Jew.
>
> Then they came for the Trade Unionists, and I didn't speak up because I wasn't a Trade Unionist.
>
> Then they came for the Catholics, and I didn't speak up because I was a Protestant.
>
> Then they came for me…and by that time there was no one left to speak up.[5]

Most of us, when we think of that dark era, are justifiably appalled and perhaps a bit judgmental. Few of us, however, think about what *we* might have done to prevent it, had we been living in that place, in that time. There were millions of Christians attending church every Sunday in Germany during the 1930s, but with only a few exceptions, they did nothing to prevent their nation's humiliation. In fact, many justified it and supported their government's policies.

We would argue that an even greater holocaust is taking place in America today with the slaughter of 1.3 million babies each year through abortion. Or take Asia—where one million women are sold into prostitution each year. It's safe to say that ours is not a world of righteousness, justice, and peace. But what do we do? How do we know when to react? On what basis do we act? How do we carve out a response consistent with our confession as a Christian?

The Awesome Power of Ideas

The ideas that created Nazism, Islam, capitalism, communism, humanism, pluralism, globalization, and even Christianity have captivated hundreds of millions.

Ideas have consequences.

Nothing results from a vacuum. Ideas produce preferences and convictions that lead to actions—shaping the destiny of the society in which we live. As the accompanying diagram illustrates, an *idea* strikes the *leaders,* who influence the *masses,* with the result that the whole *world* is changed because of an idea.

In order to penetrate the idea level of society, in order to influence the leaders (who in turn influence the masses and the world), each of us must learn to bring God's thoughts to bear on all situations, drawing our ideas and inspiration directly from His truth. Even if our spheres of influence seem small or inconsequential, ideas have a way of spreading. And if there is one thing God delights to do, it is using ordinary men and women to accomplish extraordinary things.

Ideas Have Consequences

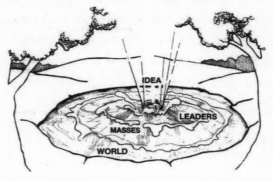

After we adopt our biblical worldview, we must begin to ask key questions. What does God's Word say about this matter or that matter? How do the overall themes of the Bible apply to this choice or decision?

Thinking with the Bible

Each of us, like a builder, needs tools to assure accuracy in what we build. Socrates is reputed to have said, "You never know a line is crooked until you have a straight one to put next to it." Without an objective, absolute, trustworthy standard, there can be no assurance of truth, no sense of confidence and certainty—about anything!

God has gifted us with an absolute standard, a straight line. He has given us His Word, the Bible, as "The Manufacturer's Handbook of Life and Living." First, it tells us about God—who He is. Second, it reveals the true origin, nature, and fall of man, as a created being who is to reflect God's image and likeness. Third, it tells us about the created world in which we have been placed as vice-regents to rule as stewards on God's behalf. Fourth, it reveals God's plan of love and forgiveness through Jesus Christ, which God established before the foundation of the world. And finally, the Bible tells us how to relate to our Creator and to other people (Matthew 22:36–40).

Failure to acknowledge that we do have a "blueprint for living" and failure to apply that blueprint lie at the root of all our problems. Too often we follow the adage, "When all else fails, read the directions." How do we know what God thinks or says about an issue if we haven't read "the handbook"?

We need to employ the attitude of the Berean church that received the words of the apostle Paul with great eagerness, "examining the Scriptures daily to see whether these things were so" (Acts 17:11). Obedience to God's holy inspired Word leads to wisdom and insight not only about our personal lives, but also about the contemporary world around us.

Tragically, most people feel that appealing to scriptural principle is old-fashioned and outdated. Yet the Bible has weathered the storms of the past and the present and stands true as our standard for life and living for the future. Billy Graham decided long ago that, rather than rely on his intelligence, wit, and emotional appeals to draw people to Christ, he would simply tell them what the Bible says and allow God's Word to prove itself.

It has. It *always* has. And it always will.

And this is a decision you can make. Once you do, it truly is like putting on those night-vision goggles; you can quickly see what glows in the dark and what does not.

Immovable, Undeniable Truth

The story is told of a massive British warship cruising the coastal waters of Ireland in the middle of a raging storm and sea. Keeping a careful watch on the storm from the bridge, the helmsman suddenly spotted the light of an oncoming ship. Summoning his captain, he apprised him of the situation. At the captain's orders, the radioman signaled the oncoming vessel. This is the transcription of the radio conversation between the British and the Irish off the coast of Kerry, October 1998:

IRISH: Please divert your course 15 degrees to the south to avoid a collision.

BRITISH: Recommend you divert your course 15 degrees to the north to avoid a collision.

IRISH: Negative. You will have to divert your course 15 degrees to the south to avoid a collision.

BRITISH: This is the Captain of a British Navy Ship. I say again, divert *your* course.

IRISH: Negative. I say again, you will have to divert *your* course.

BRITISH: THIS IS THE AIRCRAFT CARRIER HMS BRITANNIA! THE SECOND LARGEST SHIP IN THE BRITISH ATLANTIC FLEET. WE ARE ACCOMPANIED BY THREE DESTROYERS, THREE CRUISERS AND NUMEROUS SUPPORT VESSELS. I DEMAND YOU CHANGE YOUR COURSE 15 DEGREES NORTH. I SAY AGAIN, THAT IS 15 DEGREES NORTH OR COUNTER-MEASURES WILL BE UNDERTAKEN TO ENSURE THE SAFETY OF THIS SHIP.

IRISH: We are a lighthouse.... Your call.

Apocryphal or not, the story reminds us that lighthouses tend to stand firm in the tempest, even while they guide storm-tossed sailors into safe harbor. What is your light-house? It needs to be the Word of God! Certainly the Bible stands alone as a guiding light to provide the answers to basic questions essential to man's understanding of himself and his world.

Fill Your Mind with Healthy Food

One activity in particular will aid us greatly in achieving a biblical worldview and training our minds to respond rightly to the world. Today we are experiencing an explosion of secular knowledge. We need to balance that input by doing as the apostle Paul commanded: "Set your mind on the things above, not on the things that are on earth" (Colossians 3:2).

This is best accomplished through meditation.

This is not the stereotypical eastern activity popularized by Transcendental Meditation or yoga. Such forms of meditation encourage people to focus on nothing, or within themselves, on a universal power or force, or on some seemingly meaningless word. Their focus is *emptying* the mind.

The biblical concept of meditation is the idea of "chewing" as a cow chews her cud. Biblical meditation *focuses* the mind. When we meditate on God and His Word, we experience three things: intimacy with God, a renewed mind as Christ's thoughts become our thoughts, and changed behavior. As we meditate on Scripture, we allow God's thoughts to so permeate our lives that they actually become our own thoughts, resulting in new behavior patterns, solid character, and a significant destiny.

Though my (Ron) conversion to Christ affected my life dramatically, I still had trouble with my thought life. Oh, it got better, but through my childhood involvement with pornography, I had built a predisposition to impurity. As a young man, I tried memorizing Scriptures, accountability groups, fasting—even cold showers. I was truly seeking to be pure in my thoughts. But while I did grow in purity in my physical life, I faced frequent failure in the thoughts and images that occupied my soul. I grew profoundly discouraged and wondered if I could ever conquer it.

Then I heard a speaker address biblical meditation. It was a new concept to me, and one I immediately embraced (if only out of utter desperation). I memorized Colossians 3:1–17 and meditated on it four times a day (first thing in the morning, around lunch time, dinner time, and before I went to bed), and every time I was tempted to think a lustful thought.

Determined to let the Word of God transform my thinking patterns, I practiced and practiced and finally built a habit (a counter habit, really) of dwelling on the Word of God, sometimes for five minutes and many times for fifteen, thirty, or even sixty minutes at a time. I prayed these Scriptures back to God, sang them into my life, and sought to apply them to every nook and cranny of my mind.

I did this for one week and then four weeks and then three months, six months, and then at around eight months I found that my desire for purity had taken the driver's seat. God's Word—through a yielded mind and heart—had broken the back of my old oppressive thought patterns. We truly believe that this spiritual discipline is one of the greatest, yet most undertaught, principles in Christendom, and key to forming a biblical mind and heart.

Following are some suggestions to help you get started in this vital area of your life.

• Schedule time, preferably daily, to be alone so that you can concentrate.

- Select a verse or passage, one that when internalized will help you in a specific area, such as a besetting sin, a weakness, an area you have selected for growth, or an issue in your profession.
- Study the passage in context.
- Memorize it. You don't have to memorize verses in order to begin meditation, but memorization will significantly aid the process of internalization.
- Reflect on its message: What does it say about God? About you? About others?
- Visualize it. Make the truth of Scripture as vivid in your mind as possible. Those in the field of mass media understand the power of visualization: It helps viewers to see a lifestyle or product the marketers want them to buy. We need to do the same with spiritual truth. As an athlete visualizes himself performing in a sports event, we need to mentally picture ourselves winning the spiritual battles of the day. It is not the visualization that produces the results; it is simply a strong tool to aid our concentration, our understanding, and our dedication to obeying and trusting in God's Word.
- Personalize the Scripture passage and make it a prayer to God.
- Take time to be quiet, to listen to what God has to say to you, and to enjoy fellowship with Him.
- Take action, applying the commands and principles of Scripture to your life.

Analyze and Understand the Issues of Our Day

In everything we hear, view, and read, we should ask questions: What is the source of this information? What are its potential biases? What is the underlying worldview? If the information comes from an individual, what is his or her moral character? What are the surface implications? What is the root issue underlying all the symptoms? As we analyze, we begin to see that this is not necessarily "just the way things are."

To put it another way, some facets of our culture's dominant worldview are so taken for granted that we begin to think there is simply no other option, that these are part of the internal structuring of things. We need to analyze the information we receive, rather than blindly accepting all that is presented to us. An excellent way to do this is to try to determine the worldview of the people presenting the information.

James Sire explains this concept well in his book *How to Read Slowly*:

> When writers write they do so from the perspective of their own worldview. What they presuppose about themselves, God, the good life and the validity of human knowledge governs both what they say and how they say it. That is why reading with worldviews in mind (your own and that of the author) will help

you understand not only what is written in the lines but what is written between the lines—that is, what is presupposed before a pen ever reaches the page.[6]

Paying the Price to Renew the Mind

Jerry has directed several multinational corporations over the years. Though he had been a Christian for many years, he had never seriously thought about the concept of Jesus Christ as Lord of his life. A meeting with the late Francis Schaeffer caused him to reevaluate his business practices and priorities in light of his faith.

In order to formulate his own worldview, Jerry stepped down from his position and spent six months studying the Bible from Genesis to Revelation, nine to ten hours every day. "When I finished that project, I was prepared to go back into the business arena," he says.

"The time I spent studying the Bible had a dramatic influence on every area of my life. For example, I decided to do some things to help improve society, based on a biblical worldview. If we don't have more businessmen working to shore up the moral framework of society, when it collapses, nobody will do business."

Granted, not many of us have the luxury of taking a six-month break. But nearly all of us could take a weekend or more each year and some time daily to get away from the pressures of business and study the Scriptures for the purpose of clarifying our worldview. We must not rely on others to do this for us. If we do nothing, others will lead us where we may not want to go.

The warfare against Satan begins right here. With ideas. With our minds. When you have a mind renewed daily by the Holy Spirit and the Word of God, an amazing phenomenon takes place in your life.

You begin to glow in the dark.

LIVING IN THE KINGDOM OF DARKNESS	LIVING IN THE KINGDOM OF LIGHT
Unaware of the spiritual battle.	Fully engaged in defensive and offensive warfare.
Is being "squeezed into the world's mold."	Is being transformed according to God's values.
Has fluctuating standards, no straight lines.	Measures standards and behavior against the straight line of the Bible.
Sees the world only in terms of himself.	Sees the big picture.
Doesn't recognize the consequences of his ideas/actions.	Recognizes that his ideas/actions have consequences.
Doesn't realize or care that his thoughts and behavior are under the control of Satan.	Determines to bring his thoughts and behavior in line with the Bible.

ACTION STEPS

▶ Ask yourself, "What is my worldview? Where are its roots contrary to Christ and enslaved to the kingdom of darkness? What steps can I take to more fully live out a biblical worldview and live as a child of the King?" Think about your worldview in these areas: family, work, use of money and time, leisure, thought life, ministry, and conversations.

▶ Take an issue you are presently facing and apply the biblical thinking process.

▶ Analyze and understand the issue.
  ▶ Compare your analysis with the Scriptures.
  ▶ Apply your biblical perspective to the issue.

▶ Identify an area in your life you'd like to change, improve, learn about, or conquer.
  ▶ Find a Scripture verse or passage that relates to it.
  ▶ Apply the section on meditation. Meditate four times daily on that Scripture, for one week. Check the difference in your attitude and approach to the problem.

2

Shining Through

Living Righteously

▶▶*Joe was really jazzed about coaching freshman sports so close to the Mexican border where most of his students crossed every morning. Even having to teach ninth grade science put a smile on his face. His kids marveled at the rudimentary experiments he set up for them—old hat to many American-born students. It was challenging to him to reach back for the Spanish of his childhood, to be teaching kids who wore the same clothes day after day, because that was all they had. He knew he was a role model for many of them, quite possibly the one consistent* adult male in their lives. And he wasn't even that old.

He shot hoops with some of the older kids after school, played a little ball with his friends on the weekends, and now and then drove north to LA to see his family. He wasn't racking up the big bucks by any means, but his expenses were minimal…as long as his Celica held out.

One Thursday in April his principal, Ms. Cast, called him in. He barely knew her and couldn't call her by her first name yet. She'd hired him at the last minute in the fall when the previous coach/science teacher retired abruptly. Once school started there was so much to cover that they hadn't had a real conversation at all. So when she looked up from her desk as he walked in, he realized he had no idea what her agenda might be.

Motioning him to a seat in front of her desk, she got right to the point. "Joe," she said, "I don't know if you've been aware that there is a new high school opening up in North County." He wasn't. "And I don't know," she continued, "if you realize that I'm going to be leaving to open the new school." No, he didn't, he said.

"Joe, I'm building a team to join me, and I'm looking for teachers like you who really invest in the students' lives. I've seen you hanging out here after school playing ball with the ninth-grade boys. I want someone like you to come with me. It's a brand-new building. No graffiti, no rusty lockers, no worn-out grass. The kids are from more intact families, more economically sound, so that will mean more parental involvement."

The principal smiled—a smile that reached into her eyes. "And here's the best part, Joe. I want you to run the entire athletic *program. You'll have all the money you need. We might even have enough money to hire another teacher so you don't have to teach freshman science."*

Joe sat back in his seat, dazzled by the sudden attention. And though Ms. Cast went on about his opportunities, the young teacher's mind was on one thing—I can get rid of the Celica!

They talked for a while, strategized a little, dreamed together about the athletic program, and when they shook hands they had agreed that Joe would confirm his decision with her by the following weekend. They both had broad smiles and a pretty strong feeling they would be working together for years to come.

Joe left school that day without playing ball. The boys watched him drive away in his battered car. He waved finally but they'd turned away before they saw it.

He hit the interstate and exited at the Mile of Cars, driving slowly, slowly, down the road with his eye out for good deals and good wheels. He hadn't even allowed himself to think about a new car, so his mind was open to anything. All afternoon and into the evening he stopped and talked and test-drove and negotiated. At a quick dinner at Wendy's he went over all the brochures.

Friday the boys were all over him, begging him to stay after and work with them on the basketball court. He'd planned to continue his car research but he acquiesced, making sure they knew they couldn't always talk him into changing his plans.

Saturday morning he drove his rusty Celica to LA for the weekend with his parents. He walked into their tiny little house, neat and clean and great smelling, and told his mom and dad about Ms. Cast's—or rather, Elaine's—offer. They were so proud of him! They saw him rising above their own lives, making the kind of money that would ensure he could afford a house and a good wife, and be accepted in the communities of the well-to-do, the communities where some of their friends did all the yard work.

That night, stretched out in his old bed, his toes hanging off the end, Joe stared at the glowing stars and planets that were still stuck on his ceiling. What an opportunity he had before him! He smiled in the dark, yet even as he did he was aware of the beginnings of an inner struggle. He'd had them before and recognized the symptoms.

He went back over Elaine's invitation and all the plans they'd considered in her office. Something was niggling at his brain, though, and he went to sleep not nearly as excited as his mother was.

Sunday morning he joined his parents at their little church down the street. The pastor had known him since fifth grade and had been one of the more significant male role models in Joe's life. He pulled Joe off to the side after the service to catch up on things. He'd been the major reason Joe became a teacher, and Joe treasured his counsel. Walking back to his office, Joe filled him in on his present life and future opportunity. His pastor listened quietly with a small smile on his face and then spoke.

"Joe, what are you really committed to? What lights a fire in your gut? What captures your heart and your imagination? What do you really want to give your life to?"

The young man sat there quietly for a long time, taking each question in turn, trying to pinpoint the nuances of what his pastor was getting at.

When his pastor excused himself for a moment and walked

out of the room, Joe got up, too, and went to the tiny window and looked out over the patio. Thinking back over the last month, he tried to visualize the highlights. And he kept coming back to a bunch of faces, boys' faces, some grinning with mischief, some tear-stained, some angry and belligerent.

The pastor walked back into the room with two cold Cherry Cokes in hand. And Joe was ready with his answer. He spoke about "his" boys and a few of their stories, and then his mentor brought the whole discussion around to one point.

"God has given you a gift, Joe, and a perfect place to use it. He wants you to be radical for Him, to choose the way that might not make sense to the rest of the world, but gives you the opportunity to BE Him for others. Of course He can use you at the new school. But who will take your place at the old one?"

Joe left LA that afternoon in his good old Celica. She had another year in her, he was sure.

Ambassadors-at-Large

Right thinking leads to right living.

We are firmly convinced that a transformed society begins with transformed individuals, living out the principles God builds within them. As we increase our ability to think biblically we can start to live rightly. We will begin to "walk in a manner worthy of the Lord...bearing fruit in every good work," as Colossians 1:10 says.

If we are living righteously, we'll align our *actions* as well as our thoughts with the Word of God. Our life will reflect Christ in the marketplace as well as at home. There will be no distinction between the character of our private life and our public one. We will live with integrity—whole, faithful, and consistent. What you see is what you get.

And this righteous living will be evident not only in Bible study, prayer, and witnessing, but in how we treat the people whose paths we cross each day, and how we respond to opportunities to flesh out the gospel. In the course of a single day, we have so many open doors to reflect the image of God. And if we ask Him, the Holy Spirit will reveal these to us hour by hour, moment by moment.

Jesus Christ told us to seek first His kingdom, and His righteousness (Matthew 6:33). Those who seek God's kingdom *first* will experience the true joy and freedom that come with right priorities. When you examine the characters of the Bible, you find that whenever people obeyed God and took a stand for righteousness, they were joyful. When they disobeyed God, when they gave in to the standards and influences around them, they were miserable. You can see it in the infant nation of Israel when they wandered in the wilderness. You can see it in the broken heart of Peter after he had denied his Lord, and sought to return to his old occupation after the Crucifixion.

That is one of the benefits of being a citizen of God's kingdom—the promise of an abundant life. In fact, it is the most exciting life imaginable. God calls His citizens ambassadors while they are on earth.

Once on an airplane, my (Ron) seatmate asked what I did for a living. Without much thought, I used an answer I'd heard recently.

"I'm an ambassador."

"You're a what?"

"I'm an ambassador."

"What country do you represent?"

"Oh, I represent something far larger than a country."

"Okay, what *do* you represent?"

"I represent a kingdom."

"What kind of kingdom?"

"The biggest! Wherever I go, I represent the King and His kingdom. I'm an ambassador of Jesus Christ."

That exchange, a little on the unusual side for me but straight out of 2 Corinthians 5, opened up a wonderful conversation with a guy who couldn't easily escape!

Total Commitment

During the early stages of World War II, an illiterate farmer from rural midwestern America heard about the attack on Pearl Harbor. Motivated by a love for his country, he and his wife immediately left the farm and headed to the West Coast to work in the shipyards. His wife found work as a waitress to support them.

Unable to read, the farmer did not understand the meaning of the scrap of paper he received once a week at the shipyard. It was not until he had accumulated several thousand dollars in checks that he learned he was being *paid* to help save his country.[7]

That farmer was committed to doing his part for the nation, and he assumed that meant sacrificing. Nowadays in the West, such self-denial is a pretty unfamiliar concept, though it abounded in the early days of America. Yet it is a core value, a necessary focus, for glowing in the dark. Without it, it's a little too hard to remain faithful.

"Faithful" will always be tested. It's the nature of the conflict.

The terrorists of today embrace sacrifice and self-denial, and that explains their phenomenal success. In fact, they are willing to die. Many from al-Qaida and other religious and political groups believe that they are serving God, and will have greater prominence in heaven by strapping explosives to their bodies, boarding a fully populated bus, and igniting the explosives.

It's difficult to defend against people who believe they have nothing of ultimate importance to lose. The irony is that *we* are the ones who have nothing to lose—because we have already been given everything in Christ, and it is secure! And just down the road (not very far) we have a glorious heaven to enjoy, centered around Him! This is such a simple truth, but think of the freedom to love others you'll have as you grow into this reality. Think about how this inner conviction has, can, and will shape the rest of your life.

Why is it that terrorists seem to have a far higher level of commitment than most Christians? The reason is that their leadership constantly reminds its members that they are fulfilling a dream far greater than any single individual. The goal is that everything the individual does—his every waking moment, his every action—is geared toward the fulfillment of a great earthly objective, and beyond that, eternal reward.

But the original "dead man on furlough" is the Galatians 2:20 Christian: "I have been crucified with Christ and I no longer live, but Christ lives in me. The life I live in the body, I live by faith in the Son of God, who loved me and gave himself for me" (NIV). This calls us to a total commitment to Christ and His lordship, a commitment surpassing even that of the suicidal terrorists.

I (Bill) was meeting at Harvard University with one of America's great statesmen. During our time together, I laid out a plan to involve a thousand key leaders in praying for, claiming, and supporting the goal of reaching one billion souls for Christ before the year 2000.

After we talked for a while, the man responded, "I don't wear my religion on my sleeve. My religion is personal and private, and I don't talk about it."

Taken aback by this very forthright rejection, I asked the man if he was a Christian. "Yes, I am," he replied, "but I'm not a fanatic."

I pressed it. "Did it ever occur to you that it cost Jesus Christ His *life* so that you could say you're a Christian? And it cost the disciples their lives. Millions of Christians throughout the centuries have suffered and died in order to get the message of God's love and forgiveness to you. Now do you really believe that your faith in Christ is personal and private and you shouldn't talk about it?"

"No sir," the man replied. "I'm wrong."

Then he asked me to tell him what he could do about it.

J. B. Phillips understood this truth when he wrote the introduction to his modern English paraphrase of the epistles:

> The great difference between present-day Christianity and that of which we read in these letters is that to us it is primarily a performance; to them it was a real experience. We are apt to reduce the Christian religion to a code, or at best a rule of heart and life. To these men it is quite plainly the invasion of their lives by a new quality of life altogether. They do not hesitate to describe this as Christ "living in" them…. We are practically driven to accept their own explanation, which is that their little human lives had, through Christ, been linked up with the very life of God.
>
> …It is heartening to remember that this faith took root and flourished amazingly in conditions that would have killed anything less vital in a matter of weeks. These early Christians were on fire with the conviction that they had become, through Christ, literally sons of God; they were pioneers of a new humanity, founders of a new Kingdom. They still speak to us across the centuries. Perhaps if we

believed what they believed, we might achieve what they achieved.[8]

Do *you* really believe that God has ripped you out of the decay of death and given you a breathtakingly new life? This isn't just a metaphor or some clever arrangement of words! Our new life is as real (or maybe even *more* real, as it has been "linked up with the very life of God") as the blood-and-bones existence we are accustomed to calling "life."

Why should the commitment of the Christian be any less today than it was in the first century? We are citizens in the kingdom of light. Ours is the greatest and only worthwhile cause. God has literally called us to go and win the world, to make disciples of all nations, teaching them to obey all that He has commanded. The reason our nation is not greatly influenced by Christianity is that so few of us have the revolutionary lifestyle necessary to make an impact.

Art DeMoss was a man who believed in Jesus as our great Creator God and Savior. During his lifetime he built up a phenomenally successful insurance company, yet his real accomplishments lay in the commitment he had to introducing people to Jesus. Everywhere he went he told waiters, cab drivers, and businessmen about his Lord, leading literally thousands to faith in Christ.

Art and I (Bill) were having dinner one evening in Cuernavaca, Mexico. As we chatted, the maître d' came over and asked if we were satisfied with the food and service. Art immediately seized the opportunity to explain that he was in town to speak at an evangelistic campaign in a local church. He asked the maître d' if he was a Christian. The man confessed that he was not. Art then proceeded to witness to him, and within a few minutes the man bowed his head and prayed with Art as he received Christ.

The secret of Art's success in business and in witnessing for the Lord lay in the fact that, no matter what happened in his daily schedule, no matter how crowded his agenda for the day, he arose early in the morning and spent at least an hour with the Lord in prayer and reading the Scriptures.

His used his home to introduce fellow executives to Christ. He hosted dinners, often with several hundred guests on his back lawn, and brought in well-known Christian athletes, executives, and government officials to present the gospel. Literally thousands of people were introduced to Christ through his ministry, and though he passed away in 1979, his impact continues to be felt today through his wife, Nancy, and their children, all of whom are dedicated to Christ. His was a revolutionary lifestyle.

Supernatural Is Not Natural

The lifestyle of the early church leaders is what God wants for all of us. But the only way we can achieve it is by living supernaturally.

To do that, we must first *think supernaturally*. That means we need to learn to think the way God thinks. A tall order, you say? Yes, but He has given us the Scriptures for this very purpose. As we read, study, and meditate on the Bible, we begin to think in ways that go beyond our normal inclinations and boundaries.

We need to learn how great God truly is.

We need to dwell on His attributes.

We need to gain confidence in His great power and love.

We need to recognize that we are men and women of destiny.

If you belong to God through Jesus Christ, there is royal blood in your veins. *"You are a chosen race, a royal priesthood, a holy nation, a people for God's own possession"* (1 Peter 2:9). Because of who God is and who we are, we have vast power and authority, far greater than any in Satan's kingdom.

Second, this lifestyle calls for us to *pray supernaturally*. We need to experience the truth of Christ's words when He said, "If you remain in me and my words remain in you, ask whatever you wish, and it will be given you" (John 15:7, NIV). We have authority over the forces of evil, and Satan and his forces cannot prevail against us.

I (Bill) have a dear friend "as common as clay"—not brilliant, eloquent, handsome, or especially outgoing. But he is a revolutionary for God. The first time I met him, he had just witnessed to one of the top political leaders in America. The circumstances of his meeting with this leader were phenomenal, because God obviously orchestrated it. This is a man whose source of power is prayer. He spends a couple of hours a day in meaningful prayer, not just ritualistic mouthing of words or phrases, but in personal conversation with the omnipotent Creator, the God of the universe. His revolutionary, supernatural quality is that he lives a holy life, walks in the Spirit, and spends much time in the Word and in prayer.

Third, we need to *plan supernaturally*. Asking God to direct us, we must make plans so magnificent, so big, so far beyond mere human accomplishment that we are doomed to failure unless God is at work in us.

After the devastating fires in Southern California in the fall of 2003, Habitat for Humanity stepped in to help with the rebuilding for those without insurance.

Now familiar as a strategic housing solution, Habitat was founded in 1976 by Millard Fuller. A talented businessman, Fuller was so successful that he was a self-made millionaire by the age of twenty-nine. But somehow, the success left him empty.

Because of a domestic crisis, my wife and I decided to completely change our lives and to seek after what God wanted us to do. We decided when we left the business, that if we were serious about changing our lives and following God that we should make ourselves totally available for those purposes and get rid of anything that would obstruct us from being free and able to do God's work. So I sold my interest in the company to my former partner and donated literally one hundred percent of the money to various Christian ventures.[9]

In place of a new business empire, Fuller formed Habitat, based on what he called biblical economics. The firm builds homes for the poor, charging no profit and no interest, and allows people twenty years to pay. No government funds are used, but Fuller challenges people to donate money, materials, and time.

"We say that we use the economics of Jesus," says Fuller. "We believe that if you move on faith, God moves with you. Our long-range goal is to eliminate poverty housing in the world. Now that's an audacious, outrageous goal and everybody says, 'You must be crazy!' But I happen to be a professing Christian. The Bible I read says that, 'With God all things are possible.'"[10]

Fourth, we need to *love supernaturally*. Jesus told His disciples to love each other, "as I have loved you.... By this all men will know that you are my disciples, if you love one another" (John 13:34–35, NIV). Such love is humanly impossible, for He loved us enough to die for each one of us. But the fruit of the Holy Spirit is love. As we allow the Spirit to control us, love is a natural result.

In fact, the Holy Spirit's presence and power is *the* key to living supernaturally in all of life—thinking, praying, planning, and loving. It's the Spirit who teaches us about God, provides supernatural peace, guides us into all truth, and empowers us to carry out His commands. That's why Jesus was able to promise that the presence of "the Helper" would be better for His disciples than His own presence. What a promise!

Libby's husband ran off with their son's piano teacher. For years she determined to keep bitterness from taking over her heart and her face…and her four kids. Though her husband made a good salary and she only minimum wage, Libby had to pay child support when their youngest son moved in with his dad. But through the power of the Holy Spirit, Libby persevered. Steeping her mind in God's Word, she spoke positively yet honestly when asked about her life, and she humbly and gratefully moved from friend to friend when she couldn't afford a place of her own. Almost always she smiled and kept a thankful heart. And then God gave her a godly man…and a few more kids.

Living supernaturally is walking by faith in the face of seemingly insurmountable odds. We are the ones who decide, as an act of the will, whether to live supernaturally. It is a choice, based on God and what He tells us in His Word. We exercise faith when we choose to act on what He says. Like a muscle, faith increases with use. The more we choose to trust God, the more we will believe Him…and the more faith we will have to trust Him for the next situation.

Supernatural living often doesn't look impressive to the world. I (Ron) once knew a young man who lived out this principle in a very quiet way. He worked for me for a time, and I considered him well educated, highly principled, and an all-around nice guy. But he was overqualified for the position I had for him, and it became clear to both of us, finally, that it was time for him to move on.

He took off with his wife and three small children to

Dallas, determined to find a job soon and get back in the business game. But it wasn't as easy as we all thought it would be. Month after month passed and no job. Finally, he had no choice but to take a paper route and drive a school bus for a period of time. When I heard about that, I was *immensely* proud that he had been willing to humble himself to care for his young family. I will never forget what he did.

God was taking my friend on a journey to the end of his human resources. As many of us who now serve the Lord can testify, it is in this very place of emptiness and desolation that we begin to discover supernatural provision that strengthens our faith like nothing else.

But there is one more point that incorporates all of supernatural living. In fact, it is the ultimate demonstration of supernatural living: becoming a bondslave of Jesus Christ.

The Life of a Contemporary Slave

The greatest experience of Vonette's and my (Bill) life occurred in 1951 when we chose to become slaves of Jesus Christ, turning over ownership of our lives and all our possessions to Him. We had to face up to the challenge of the Lord Jesus when He said, "Seek first the kingdom of God and His righteousness" (Matthew 6:33, NKJV), and "Do not lay up for yourselves treasures upon earth, where moth and rust destroy and where thieves break in and steal; but lay up for yourselves treasures in heaven" (Matthew 6:19–20, NKJV).

I was a very materialistic person, and so was my wife. We had an appetite for luxury. I was in business for myself, enjoyed the good life, and had great prospects for a life of exceptional financial success. I manufactured fancy foods; was involved in leasing, drilling, and producing oil in the Midwest; and was already experiencing considerable return on my investments. As a believer, I planned to give a good percentage of my profits to the Lord.

But the Lord had something else in mind.

In the spring of 1951, He led Vonette and me to sign a contract with Him, whereby we formally became slaves of Jesus Christ, just as Paul speaks of in Romans 1:1:

Paul, a bond-servant of Christ Jesus, called as an apostle, set apart for the gospel of God....

James, Peter, John, and Jude speak of themselves in the same way. So we chose to relinquish all of our rights to Him—and put it in writing. In this same document, we pledged never to seek the praise or applause of men, labor for material wealth, or pursue the worldly lifestyle that had once been so important to us. It was our goal simply to be slaves of Jesus Christ the rest of our lives, to do whatever He wanted us to do, to go wherever He wanted us to go, whatever the cost, and say whatever He wanted us to say.

It was soon after that commitment that God revealed the vision that led to the formation of Campus Crusade for Christ. I do not believe that God would have entrusted me with the vision for this ministry had there not first been our total surrender to the lordship of Christ.

Many of us have no problem considering ourselves servants of God. But slaves? Now that's a different matter. Yet there are some distinct advantages to being a slave as opposed to being a servant.

A servant is paid a wage, though sometimes it's not a great amount. With that money, he is free to do what he wishes, but he also has the responsibility for obtaining his own food, shelter, clothing, and any other possessions. A slave, however, is not paid any wage. The master is responsible for providing all that the slave needs. The slave has no responsibility except to do what the master tells him to do. The master may reward him for a job well done, and sometimes that turns out to be more than a servant would have earned. But the slave never expects such blessing.

The servant works a certain number of hours, and then he has his own time to do as he pleases. The slave is always at the call of his master. His time is never his own; but whatever the master desires, the slave gladly obliges.

One might wonder why anyone would want to be a slave. The apostle Paul considered himself a slave and derived great joy from wearing the label. The Greek word he used several times is *doulos*. It's a term used for both common slaves and the imperial or royal slaves of kings and emperors, who often had more authority than ordinary citizens.

Paul saw himself as no mere bondslave—one who could work off his debt and obtain freedom after seven years. The apostle likened himself to a slave who *freely chose* to be a slave. Under Hebrew law, a freed slave could then ask the master to mark him as belonging to the master's household, becoming a shareholder in the master's estate. That was Paul's attitude in choosing to become a slave of Jesus.

Vonette and I (Bill) became so totally convinced of the wisdom of this choice that we ordered our gravestones to be engraved with the words: "Slaves of Jesus."

And so Jesus challenged His disciples, "If anyone wishes to come after Me, he must deny himself, and take up his cross and follow Me" (Matthew 16:24). Paul, because of the overwhelming love God showed him, chose to become God's slave. That same opportunity awaits us.

Adventurous Lifestyle

What does a slave of Jesus look like? He or she is anyone who is committed to doing God's will in every area of life—in business or profession, in family, in church, in his neighborhood, and in the world.

> I am part of the "Fellowship of the Unashamed."
> The die has been cast. I have stepped over the line.
> The decision has been made.
> I am a disciple of Jesus Christ.
> I won't look back, let up, slow down,
> back away, or be still.

My past is redeemed, my present makes sense,
and my future is secure.
I am finished and done with low living,
sight walking, small planning,
smooth knees, colorless dreams, chintzy giving,
and dwarfed goals.
I no longer need preeminence, prosperity, position,
promotions, plaudits, or popularity.
I now live by presence, lean by faith,
love by patience,
lift by prayer, labor by power.
My pace is set, my gait is fast, my goal is heaven,
my road is narrow, my way is rough,
my companions few, my God reliable,
my mission clear.
I cannot be bought, compromised, deterred,
lured away, turned back, diluted, or delayed.
I will not flinch in the face of sacrifice,
hesitate in the presence of adversity,
negotiate at the table of the enemy,
ponder at the pool of popularity,
or meander in the maze of mediocrity.
I am a disciple of Jesus Christ.
I must go until Heaven returns,
give until I drop, preach until all know,
and work until He comes.
And when He comes to get His own,
He will have no problem recognizing me.
My colors will be clear.[11]

LIVING IN THE KINGDOM OF DARKNESS	LIVING IN THE KINGDOM OF LIGHT
Relies on self	Depends on God
Lives in the natural realm	Lives supernaturally
Life is drudgery, mere existence	Life is a spiritual adventure
Rules own life	Slave of Christ

ACTION STEPS

▸ Reread the opening story about Joe. How did he demonstrate a radical and committed life for Christ? How could you?

▸ As an "ambassador for Christ," how should your life be different—thoughts, words, actions, faith, attitude, relationships, etc? Be specific and paint an ideal picture.

▸ How do you react to J. B. Phillips's comments comparing first-century to present-day Christianity? Where would your life align with the first century? How about your family? Your church?

▸ What one element of each—supernatural living and being a slave—do you need to apply?

3

Passing the Torch

Building a Healthy Family

▶▶ *Out of the corner of his eye, Ramon noticed a little too much smoke escaping from his covered barbecue. He set down his coffee and rushed outside to check the burgers, flipping the ones in the center and rearranging all twelve to make sure they cooked evenly. He knew how each one in his family liked their burger, but tonight, with none of them here yet, beggars could not be choosers!*

Next door, Ramon could hear their young neighbors, Sam and Marcie, beginning their own barbecue. It crossed his mind that he could invite them over, but with his kids coming with their kids…well, it just seemed a little much.

His wife, Jackie, had stopped at the store on her way home from the hospital. Changing out of her nurse's uniform, she was now busy slicing tomatoes and onions, and browning some mushrooms on the stove. Those kids better get here, he thought. And just then he heard some whoops and hollers from the front of the house, and the slam of numerous car doors.

The kids and grandkids spilled into the backyard, Ramon's daughters stopping on their way to drop off their contributions to dinner in the kitchen. As Ramon saw them coming toward him, one by one, it hit him again, as it always did when they were all together, how blessed he was that his kids genuinely liked each other and their parents, and made it a point to be together frequently. Scooping up little Ramona in his arms, he spun around and around, nuzzling whiskered kisses into the back of her soft tiny neck.

And out of the corner of his eye, he saw Sam and Marcie peering over the fence.

Oh, what the heck, he thought. "Sam! Marcie! Why don't you guys come over here for dinner tonight? You'll have to bring your own meat, though."

Sam and Marcie gladly accepted the invitation. It was a little too quiet at their house, and Ramon and his loud, loving family intrigued them.

The weather was beautiful, and with dark falling later and later, the neighbors sat comfortably for several hours talking about all sorts of things and watching the children run through the sprinklers. Around nine, Ramon's kids began to gather their own children, collect all the abandoned shoes and toys, and one by one they left the way they'd come, with smiles on their faces and words of love.

But Marcie and Sam lingered, wanting to talk a little bit more. Jackie made a fresh pot of decaf and brought out a couple of stadium blankets to wrap around chilly shoulders and knees. Sam began by expressing his thanks for the evening, but before he'd finished that short sentiment Marcie's eyes filled with tears. Jackie, ever the mother, noticed at once, scooted her chair closer to Marcie's, and put a strong, comforting arm around her shoulders. Sam was clearly uncomfortable with Marcie's emotion and tried to divert the attention. Eventually, however, and with coaxing, they began to talk.

For five years they had enjoyed their lives together. They weren't making tons of money, but their rent wasn't too bad and their car was paid off. Their jobs were okay for the time being, and they had lots of friends.

Before they were married, they'd decided not to bring children into such an unstable world, but they were beginning to suspect that it wasn't the children they were protecting as much as themselves.

Now Marcie was feeling a tugging on her heart to have at least one child. Her friends were mothers several times over, and she'd spent too much time at the park watching bewitching two-year-olds playing in the sand not to want one. Sam hadn't had such experiences. He was an only child of an only child and around other people's children just long enough to see what trouble they could be. He didn't want to be a father.

Yet he had to admit there was something rather wonderful about Jackie and Ramon's family. Something life giving. Something energizing. And, albeit reluctantly, he was finally ready to talk about it.

For another hour Sam and Marcie grilled their older neighbors about kids and childbirth and money and the future in general. Ramon and Jackie weren't even tempted to steer the conversation away from the hard stuff. With openness and honesty they recounted some of the challenging stories that had helped to define and strengthen their family...and they finished the conversation with some hilarious moments as well.

When they walked home, silently hand in hand, Sam and Marcie were thinking thoughts they'd never thought before.

About a guest room that might work as a nursery.

Taking Up the Gauntlet

God has put within all his children a compelling need to connect exclusively with a family. It's why sailors tattoo "Mom" on their biceps; it's why June is busting out all over with weddings; it's why singles long to be included during the holidays.

The family is the smallest of groups, the initial "institution" God created, what He deemed as the perfect place to display His relationship within Himself. Yet the traditional family is under attack. Marriages worldwide are torn apart by public laws that encourage separation, easy divorce laws that minimize commitment, and even by a redefinition of "family." Even the Christian world, long the standard-bearer of healthy family living, reels with brokenness. Unbelievably, the divorce rate in Christian marriages has now *surpassed* that of the general public.

Too many children are born and reared for their value to the economics or status of the family rather than the perpetuation of any set of values or altruistic purposes—or they're unplanned, unwanted, and abandoned altogether. Some couples, perhaps to avoid the stress, risk, or expense of children, are avoiding the opportunity completely. And some couples, in God's providence, even though they long for kids of their own, cannot have children and are often blind to the incomparable impact they might have as friends and mentors to other people's kids.

Field Hospital

There is no more obvious example of both the spoils and casualty of war than the family. Families can seem like warm, secure cocoons or rock-hard granite. They have the potential of reaping the greatest of rewards—love, security, comfort, support, prayer, understanding—or suffering the most profound of sorrows—insecurity, suspicion, ingratitude, betrayal, rejection, pain, loneliness.

But as with any discouraging trend, the bad news for the family has created for those of us with a biblical worldview a very clear and compelling mandate to lead the way to change. The darker it grows, the brighter the light shines in contrast. As we intentionally develop a habit of thinking with Scripture and the practice of living revolutionary, sold-out lives, we must prepare our families defensively and offensively, both to withstand the assault of the enemy and also to lead the charge against him.

The family should be a place of *triage* (diagnosis), *operation* (the initial hard work), and *recovery* (when the healing takes place).

Mary and I (Ron) had breakfast with a young couple recently just about ready to have their first baby. They've been married nearly three years and work together in a new and very successful business. We sat high up on a hotel rooftop patio overlooking the Pacific Ocean talking about interdependence versus codependence in a marriage. They were trying to distinguish between the two and trying to build new habit patterns for their relationship. She had grown up in a home where she was her mother's enabler, where the men in her life were not to be depended upon, and she married a young man who was finding it difficult to convince her he could be trusted.

As we talked, it became very clear that they are working hard to erase the negative impact of their birth families while holding on to the positive things. And all the while, as they ask questions and read books and get counseling, they grow closer and closer.

In the process, they're getting ready to glow in the dark.

You can see it in their eyes.

They are experiencing the "field hospital" aspect of family. Their young faces and eager expectation that this current struggle has a purpose and an end are evidence that they are working out of a biblical worldview and are well aware of the battle. Theirs will be a home of healing. I can't wait to see what the Spirit of God does under this roof.

Oh, that our homes would so reflect the love of Christ and the biblical understanding of the value of each human life that everyone walking through our front door would feel loved, accepted, and safe! The apostle John said the world will know we are followers of Christ by the love we have for one another. That is our charge.

We want our children and grandchildren to feel that love and to know they are always welcome and wanted at home. We want to create the kind of atmosphere that enables them to share struggles and victories and know we won't overreact. We also want to be available to their friends and our friends as a place of security. And we want our neighbors to know that we are available for whatever they need.

Mary and I invited a missionary family to live with us for a year when our own children left for college. Yes, we were responding to their need, and yes, we were also reluctant to face our empty nest! The father in this family needed time and space to heal from an illness he had picked up overseas, the mother needed support and love while she ran the family, and the children needed a little extra security. All we did was be a family with these precious friends. We had fingerprints on the sliding glass doors again and refrigerator art and toys strewn down the stairs. But we loved it. The family spirit was rich and powerful, and we all felt it.

We know of one couple that was suffering deeply because of some poor choices in their separate and collective pasts and the pressures of living a public life. Two other couples, just friends really, came to them and formed a protective circle around them, nursing them through months of physical, mental, and spiritual pain, and shielding them from having to explain their problems to too many people.

It took nearly a year of frequent counseling, get-togethers, and hand-holding, lots of tears and anger and grief, until finally the healing took hold and they came out the other side—strong, joyful, growing, clear-headed, hopeful and in a position to help others. It was hard work and worth every gut-wrenching moment for all involved.

There are hurting souls all around us. Within a stone's throw of where you live. Or maybe under your own roof. Some are victims of others' poor behavior and some have themselves to blame. But all need the hand of love and mercy extended to them.

Paul exhorts us along with the believers in Thessalonica to "warn those who are idle, encourage the timid, help the weak, be patient with everyone" (1 Thessalonians 5:14, NIV).

This verse confirms that a "one size fits all" approach to connecting with the hurting will not work. There is one common attitude, though, of love and mercy with the continuing undercurrent of, "There but for the grace of God go I."

Our challenge as a community of believers is to ensure that no one is left out on the battlefield, either intentionally or unintentionally. The Bible supports the notion that when there is no nuclear family nearby, the body of Christ needs to step in and provide the same environment for singles, orphans, widows, and others without familial support.

Look around you. Are there singles in your circle of acquaintances who might like a local family connection? Are there widows who need someone to change their oil or drive them to the gym? Are there single parents who could use another adult influence on their children?

All believers are members of the body of Christ. While not blood relatives, we are related by the blood of Christ and responsible for caring for one another. If we take this seriously and live like it's true, we will be much more mindful and aware of others' needs.

The Family: Basic Training Center

I (Ron) have been working with a top executive in a burgeoning technology company. Executives in his field, himself included, are accustomed to working ten- to twelve-hour days, six to seven days a week, just to keep on top of things.

We were working through a discussion on priorities one day and spent quite a bit of time talking about what lasts and what *doesn't*. I could tell he was gritting his teeth when we came to the part where I asked him to make some very hard choices: What could he do to continue to convince his wife and children that they are truly his top priority? How could he tweak his schedule so he'd have enough time to be excellent in his profession *and* romance his wife? What did he need to change so his kids never feel neglected?

It was an easy sell that did not make for easy, flippant choices. But somehow, once he settled in his mind, and out loud, what the consequences were of *not* facing this priority assessment head on, he was ready to make some changes in his life. Number one, he committed to closing down his offices on the weekends, unlike the other professionals in his field. Second, rather than hit-or-miss date nights with his wife, he committed to one night every week just for her. And third, he takes off every Tuesday after lunch for the rest of the day to have a date with one of his kids.

It almost takes one's breath away to think of the business he turns away with such a schedule. And yes, his bottom line is affected…but not in the way you might imagine. Not only are his wife and children feeling significantly more important to him, his business has taken off. Somehow, in God's economy, less is more. Could he have more creative energy because he is rested? Could his spirit feel free because he is confident there is balance in his life? Is he a better boss because he is a better husband and father? Does his very presence convey confidence rather than hectic living? God has blessed his decisions to put things in order in ways he never dreamed.

Can you imagine what this says to his family, to his

friends, and to his co-workers? He's taking the kind of leadership in his home that every man is created to take, regardless of ability, education, or wealth. And while he's pouring attention into his children's hearts and shaping their understanding of God by doing so, he's also showing them that right priorities bring blessing.

Fortune magazine ran a cover headline that read: "Why Do 'Grade A' Executives Get an 'F' as Parents?" It's a common problem for executives and their families. But I can guarantee you *this* man's grade point is on the rise.

The lesson isn't, "Tell your boss you're taking Tuesday afternoons off." It's "examine your life" to see what changes you can make to uplift your spouse and your children.

Because families are training centers for parents as well. Every day we are learners in one sense or another. And our families are specially designed to teach us so many lessons— how to love unconditionally, what it means to "die to self," how to care for the hurting, the importance of patience and gentleness...and then how to give that away to the world around us.

The "One Anothers"

We are not ashamed to reiterate without reservation that the Bible is the one consistently dependable "straight line," a historically legitimate textbook on relationships and character. It is also God's best communication, description, and instruction to us on the family. It's where we look to find the tactical battle plan. It's the guide to our inside-out obedience and transformation.

As a new Christian in 1946, I (Bill) heard my pastor quote statistics concerning marriage that had a profound impact on me. Where as many as one in two-and-a-half marriages ended in divorce at that time, he had found that among husbands and wives who *read the Bible and prayed together every day*, only one in 1,015 marriages ended in divorce! Though the numbers are significantly higher in the divorce category today, the relative statistics remain the same.

With the impact of the Bible in mind, we would like to offer up a set of strategies with which to train our families. Over 150 commands known as the "one another" passages are peppered throughout the New Testament, particularly in the letters of Paul to the churches. These are directives concerning how God's people are to live together—love one another, bear one another's burdens, pray for one another, encourage one another—and they have implications in our marriages, with our children, and in our outside relationships as well.

We believe that healthy marriages and parent/child relationships must be grounded upon these "one another" passages. As we consider our spouses and children as "one anothers," we will realize how important it is to learn and apply the whole of Scripture to these significant relationships.

In the context of the most intimate community created by

God, our first great task is to learn how to treat one another and in so doing build our character. Our greatest defense lies there.

"On husbands…"

Ephesians 5:25 says, "Husbands, love your wives, just as Christ also loved the church and gave Himself up for her." What does that look like? It looks like Galatians 5:13 (NIV: "serve one another in love"), Romans 15:7 ("accept one another"), and Ephesians 4:32 (NIV: "Be kind and compassionate to one another").

Robertson McQuilkin, President Emeritus of Columbia Bible College, left his respected academic position to care for his wife, afflicted with Alzheimer's disease at a relatively young age. He writes in *A Promise Kept*,

> The decision was made [to leave], in a way, forty-two years ago when I promised to care for Muriel "in sickness and in health…till death do us part." …Even in this loss, however, I made a wonderful discovery. As Muriel became ever more dependent on me, our love seeped to deeper, unknown crevices of the heart…. My imprisonment turned out to be a delightful liberation to love more fully than I had ever known. We found the chains of confining circumstance to be, not instruments of torture, but bonds to hold us closer.[12]

Contrast Robertson McQuilkin with one leading pastor forced to come to grips with his poor leadership in his home. After twenty-two consecutive nights out, his distraught wife asked him, "Do you *really* need to go? Can't you stay home one night?"

At that, he turned to her and said, "Fine! People are going to hell all around us! We can help them by doing God's work, and you want me to stay home and hold your hand!" His wife didn't need to say anything after that. His own statement rebuked him.

"And wives..."

Ephesians 5 exhorts wives to submit to and respect their husbands. The passage *also* says, "be kind and compassionate to one another," "forgive each other," and "be patient." The New Testament is rife with specific examples and mandates about how wives should treat the men in their lives.

What does submission look like? It's really just the "one anothers" strung together. It's offering the kindness and compassion of Ephesians to your husband by seeking to understand him. It means forgiving him when he forgets your anniversary, and being patient when he goes to the store and brings back everything but what you asked him to get in the first place. It means building him up in public in front of your friends and in private in front of your children. It means honoring him as the head of the household, lining yourself up under his leadership and recognizing that as a place of protection and security. And yes, it also means serving him—as he is to serve you—putting his needs and those of your children in front of your own.

Paul lays the cornerstone for all the "one another" verses in Philippians 2:3 (NIV): "Do nothing out of selfish ambition or vain conceit, but in humility consider others better than yourselves." Couples who choose to relate to each other in this selfless way build marriages that shout to the world, drawing attention to a way of thinking and acting that is a far cry from the selfish living around us.

"You singles…"
Then there are those close-knit groups of single friends who, until they marry or because they won't, live as a community in many ways akin to an extended family. To you we say care for each other in the way of the "one anothers." You, too, have a call and an opportunity to speak to the world by how you treat one another, how you live in community, and how you relate to the nuclear families around you. Study those passages. Learn to live with housemates, being "devoted to one another" while you "submit to one another out of reverence for Christ"…"in humility consider[ing] others better than yourselves" (Romans 12:10; Ephesians 5:21; Philippians 2:3, NIV).

"What about the kids?"

Imagine the strength of your relationships with your children if the "one anothers" become part of your strategy for raising them. Look ahead to the adults they will become, shaped by truths they can use the rest of their lives. Teach your children James 5:9 (NIV), "don't grumble against each other," and James 5:16 (NIV), "pray for each other," and as they grow they'll be able to use those skills at school and in any jobs they hold.

Prompt them, as Paul did the Thessalonians, to build each other up and to encourage each other. If you do, you will be preparing your children to be good friends, faithful spouses, and staunch defenders of the family. Teach them their responsibility to participate in their own character development, and you will be preparing them for the future.

When my (Ron) son Matt was a little boy, I knew I wanted to begin building his character as early as I could. The book of Proverbs seemed the best place to start so I bought Matt a children's *Living Bible* and we went to Bob's Big Boy weekly to work through Proverbs verse by verse, using colored highlighters to note what it said about various areas: the tongue (yellow), wisdom/heart (red), prohibitions/sins (blue), and good actions (green). He was only six years old when we began. Later, Matt went through on his own and listed all the verses on wisdom. This type of self-learning established a base for godly conviction in Matt's life.

It came in handy when he was struggling with a habit of complaining. Because of what he'd seen in Proverbs, I was able to appeal to his desire to be a "man of wisdom." So together we did a Bible study on thanksgiving (as the most effective alternative to complaining) and worked up this acrostic:

Trust God for everything (Philippians 4:6).
Honor the Lord (Revelation 5:13).
Acknowledge God's goodness (1 Corinthians 1:4;
    Psalm 145).
Never grumble or gripe (Philippians 2:14–15).
Know God's blessings (Psalm 146).
Sing a song of praise (Psalm 149:1).
Give thanks in everything (1 Thessalonians 5:18).
Instantly give thanks (Ephesians 5:20).
Verbalize your praise (1 Corinthians 14:16–19).
Input positive thoughts in your mind (Philippians 4:8).
Need the Holy Spirit (Galatians 5:25;
    Ephesians 5:18–20).
Grow in gratitude (Philippians 4:8).

Over the years this study on thanksgiving has been a key element in Matt's life, but more importantly, he has become a student of the Bible. And it all started at Bob's Big Boy.

Recently my wife and I (Ron) received an e-mail from a friend whose husband happened to be out of town for the weekend when she was presented with that notorious culprit, the deceptive teenager.

"Pray for me," she wrote. "I had to put Eric on restriction

for the first time. He's missing a *really fun* party for his team. It's at his best friend's house, and all the team is going. But while on vacation, he bought some stuff he wasn't supposed to, hid it, and got caught (by me). We are disciplining him for deception and lack of trust. He's at the age of succumbing to peer pressure because the results of disobeying mom and dad haven't been more painful than the pressure of not doing what the crowd wants. So we are upping the ante on 'painful.' It is hurting me way more than him. I could use your prayers, and so could Eric that he would do the right thing and his heart would be open to the discipline. He is at the age where he's 'saved' but he's not willing to 'go against the flow' for what is right. He thinks my standards are too high and that 'everybody's doing it.' I have all the 'right answers' for him, but it's his heart that needs to be open to wanting to hear them."

Our greatest hope for all our children is that they will learn to live in light of what is written in the Word of God, becoming strong enough to swim against the current of popular opinion. As parents, we must stick to the principles we know are true. That's when our kids begin to learn the deep truths of righteous behavior.

This mom's update: "Thanks for praying. Things are going well, so far. Eric has taken his restriction well and he and his dad had a long talk...."

Families shaped by the "one anothers" in the Bible (and by all the other relevant passages we tend to overlook because they don't give specific direction to husbands, wives, or children) are strong enough to withstand outside forces. At the same time, however, they are pliable enough to live in the world without being taken in by it, and are prepared for battle with an enemy whose chosen tactic is to split families.

God's Bigger Plan

The family needs to act as a *transformer*—intentionally having a kingdom impact.

All these examples of caring for one another must result in more than a growing family or committed friendships. It's so easy to remain in our safe relationships, even when they require a lot of us, because there is a sense of safety in the familiar.

God has a bigger plan.

As war continues to surge all around us, He expects us to take our part in defeating the kingdom of darkness and bringing light to our generation and those behind us. That's passing the torch. That's glowing in the dark.

While training and triage are large parts of our preparation and without them we are made weak and ineffective, they are just that—preparation. We are preparing our children to stand strong and long for truth and righteousness, and make a difference in their communities. We are strengthening our marriages so they won't be casualties, but will rather become magnets to the hurting marriages around us. And when people come to our door, or stop us in the grocery store, or visit our church, and ask, "What's your secret?" we must have an answer for what they see.

First, the members of a family need to agree that there is a bigger purpose for their lives.

The contract with God that Vonette and I (Bill) signed many years ago was a statement of an absolute, irrevocable commitment to the lordship of Christ in our lives. It was our purpose statement as a couple. It shaped the choices we made, how we raised our children, and how we spent our money and our time.

And it has proved sufficient in all the seasons of our lives. When our boys, Zac and Brad, were small, Vonette felt pushed and frustrated because she wanted to involve herself fully in Campus Crusade for Christ. After the children were born, she had to adjust to her new situation and responsibilities.

I finally said to her, "Honey, if you will make it your priority to keep the house running, and make the boys happy and see that their needs are met, that will be the most important thing you can do *now*."

That relieved Vonette of a burden, because she realized a time would come when the boys would not need a mother at home and the house would not need a full-time homemaker; then she could concentrate on her role as a full-time partner with me in the ministry of Campus Crusade.

Since the boys have grown up and married, Vonette has been able to serve God within Campus Crusade, as well as develop the Great Commission Prayer Crusade, co-chair the International Prayer Assembly in Korea in 1984, serve on the

Lausanne Committee for World Evangelization, and even introduce legislation in Congress in 1988 (unanimously approved) to make the first Thursday of May the yearly National Day of Prayer. Today, in addition to her travel and speaking, Vonette puts together a one-minute daily radio address through which she encourages women to impact their world with Christ, and she has published several books.

Vonette was content that God had a time and place for her ministry in the home in earlier years with more time of ministry outside the home in later years. God honored her obedience in caring for the needs of our sons and home. Now she has one of the most effective women's ministries in the world.

Second, the family as a group and individually should be reaching out to win people to Christ and stimulate believers to grow. Once a family is growing in health and godliness, it is freed to help others grow.

Jim and Debi Godsey were ready to dissolve their marriage in 1990. A lifestyle of childhood abuse, addictions, and pain—and all the consequences that come with such a history—left them sick and hopeless. Debi was so desperate for some peace she had decided to shoot both Jim and herself the day the divorce was final.

But God has ways of getting through to us that few can predict. An old drinking friend of Debi's insisted she and Jim attend a weekend marriage seminar put on by FamilyLife (a ministry of Campus Crusade for Christ). Twelve days before the divorce, they went, not expecting any kind of miracle.

But a miracle occurred, just the same.

Back in their room, after hearing about God's love and forgiveness and His plan for marriage, Debi turned to Jim and began to apologize. At the same time, Jim poured out an apology to her. Miraculously, God dealt with their past, present, and future right then and there.

The Godseys are leading a revolutionary lifestyle and having a powerful kingdom impact. They took their newfound faith and hope and began giving it out to single moms and their children, and to others whose lives have fallen apart. They began a ministry they call "God's Kidz in the Hood," and have been instrumental in restoring families. Kids have come to Christ, lives have been saved, and relationships have been healed.

"For everyone to whom much is given, from him much will be required," the Scriptures say (Luke 12:48, NKJV). We all have the wherewithal, the mandate, and the example to offer to others on behalf of Christ the love and forgiveness He's given us.

We know families who pray regularly over the countries of the world for the light to penetrate and many to come to Christ.

We know families who pray over every Christmas card they receive that those families will know Christ as their Savior.

We know families who walk their neighborhood and pray for the salvation of their neighbors, those they know, and those they don't.

We know families who invite neighbors to "discussion

dinners" where they talk over issues of the day and set the stage for the gospel.

We know families who invite their neighbors to HomeBuilders[13] studies where they learn together what it means to have a godly home.

We know families who invite the entire *community* to hear a well-known figure speak about his faith.

Simple hospitality often opens the door for ministry. Both of our families are comfortable with hospitality in one form or another, partly because we've had the room over the years. But that's not the point. We are all commanded to love one another, and our homes are prime environments for such love to be demonstrated. "Offer hospitality to one another without grumbling" (1 Peter 4:9, NIV).

The computer thesaurus listed these four synonyms for hospitality: welcome, warmth, kindness, and generosity. These qualities, these expressions of love, are all that's needed, and they can be demonstrated in such simple ways. Cookies for newcomers, dog sitting for vacationers, barbecues on Memorial Day, dinners for the sick. Carpools, babysitting, mail-gathering, Christmas parties, yard clean-up days, baby showers. Even buying the neighborhood kids' fund-raising candy bars.

Mary and I (Ron) were amazed to see what God did through our son in his senior year of high school. Deeply impressed by a visit to a Promise Keepers event in Colorado, Matt took it upon himself to gather a bunch of kids to pray on Sunday afternoons at our house. The one requirement was clear: The group was open to anyone who wanted to pray to the God of the Bible. They followed a simple A-C-T-S model (adoration, confession, thanksgiving, supplication).

While the group was small and tight-knit during the fall semester, after Christmas it exploded, often with fifteen to twenty people attending on a weekend. And most of these kids weren't believers. One had a Buddhist background. Some were lapsed Catholics or California agnostics. But there they were, praying for a long time (usually forty-five minutes to an hour), praising the Lord, confessing sins, and interceding for one another. Out of that group came kids whose hearts were profoundly shaped by a bunch of other kids who loved them sins and all. Many had a newfound understanding of the attributes of the one true God. And some went on to total dependence upon our Great Creator and Savior, Jesus Christ.

A Family That Glows

Alberto and Debbie have a passion for families and reconciliation.

And it's a good thing they do, because through a crazy set of circumstances they added ten children to their family of five.

Here's the explanation: In 2003, their family took an afternoon to help a grandmother they didn't even know with her ten grandkids, who were losing their mother to cancer and their father to jail. Watching the chaos in this tiny house, they offered to help however they could. "Would you take some of the children?" the grandmother asked.

That wasn't exactly what they'd had in mind!

That plaintive cry for help, however, began what will be a lifetime of blessing and heartache, victories, and setbacks. "They were living in such darkness. We see it as spiritual warfare for the souls and legacy of these ten kids."

The children, ages six months to fourteen years, lived with Alberto and Debbie for several months, but Debbie knew that in order to experience normal life and growth, the kids needed the example and attention of smaller families. Now ten families in their church—fifty-seven people—are involved.

Alberto and Debbie are temporary guardians for all ten children and are rearing the baby, Nicholas, with their own three children. They are overseeing the legal battles, trying to keep the children from the state's foster care system, making sure kids and caretakers alike have ample opportunities to talk to counselors and each other, and holding this community together through birthday parties, picnics, monthly meetings—and an occasional bowling night.

They are tired, stretched emotionally and financially, and frustrated with a sometimes intractable bureaucracy. Not to mention the fact that the little baby is now a two-year-old nonstop motion machine. Yet asked if they would do it again, Debbie says yes. "God wanted us to step in." Speaking for this group, but specifically for themselves, Debbie says, "They'll be our kids forever. They're here to stay."

Here's the bottom line. God has established the family as

one of the foundational institutions upon which society rests. If the foundation crumbles, the whole of society disintegrates. When the foundation remains strong and withstands outside forces, it becomes a shelter for the hurting, confused, and lonely...and the proud, selfish, and independent. And, finally, it becomes a loudspeaker to the world.

In fact, it glows in the dark.

VIEW OF THE KINGDOM OF DARKNESS	VIEW OF THE KINGDOM OF LIGHT
Husbands, wives, and children live independent lives, and a strong family is simply one that gets along.	Husbands, wives, and children are committed to caring for one another and bearing one another's burdens together.
Husband pursues career goals and minimizes his family responsibilities. He focuses on what his wife is or is not doing for him.	Husband is the shepherd of his family and gives his life for wife and family.
Wife resists her husband's authority and focuses on what her husband is or is not doing for her.	Wife joyfully submits to her husband's position, enjoying his protection and recognizing both his authority and her equal worth.
Both find their primary fulfillment outside the home.	Both find their primary fulfillment within the home.

VIEW OF THE KINGDOM OF DARKNESS	VIEW OF THE KINGDOM OF LIGHT
Husbands/fathers have responsibilities in the family but give little personal leadership.	Husbands/fathers lead well in providing for spiritual as well as physical needs.
Parents tend to see children as a liability and an obstacle to fulfilling their own desires.	Parents embrace children as a gift of God and an opportunity to invest their lives in a future godly generation.
Parents relegate the upbringing of their children to babysitters, day care centers, television, or leave them without supervision.	Parents take every possible opportunity to fulfill their responsibility to care for and train their children, and shape their character.
Parents refuse to discipline a child; it will make a violent person.	Parents discipline lovingly, helping direct the will of the child to obey the authorities God puts over him.
Home is where my needs come first.	Home is a place of healing, where the focus is on caring for one another.
Homes are castles, closed off from the world, afraid of infection.	Homes are open, inviting people in (with appropriate boundaries) for the sake of healing and transformation.
Families live for themselves.	Families live for others, seeking to make an intentional kingdom impact.

ACTION STEPS

▸ Do you think we as a culture are winning or losing the battle for the family?

▸ If you picked up the gauntlet for your family, what would that look like—attitudes, behavior, words, schedules, etc.?

▸ What activity needs to be added or subtracted in your family? What can you do now?

▸ Does biblical training take place in your home? Pollster George Barna reports that 90 percent of Christian parents say they have the primary responsibility for the spiritual formation of their children. What specifically can you do here?

▸ What specific steps can you and your family take to have an impact on the world, i.e. glow in the dark?

4

City on a Hill

Building a Healthy Church

▶▶ *Bobby and Tina couldn't have been happier. Life was working out exactly according to the plan they'd laid out six months earlier, just before their wedding. Tina's job at the* San Diego Union-Tribune *gave her plenty of challenge, tapping into her extraordinary gifts. She was feeling fulfilled and stretched all at once. Bobby was newly drafted by the San Diego Padres, not the strongest team in the league but sporting a brand-new baseball park that rivaled the best in the world. They'd put together enough of their own cash and some family gifts and loans to buy a little house twenty minutes from both their jobs. The traffic was a little* more of an issue than they thought it would be; but still they had plenty of time together. They were happy, middle-class newlyweds with a promising future.

Then Tina got pregnant. Three years before "the plan." Before they were really settled in their new home. Before their finances were where they wanted them to be. They didn't tell anyone, even though Tina couldn't look at food before noon, and the pulsating screen saver on her monitor made her dizzy until she changed it for a static image of Stonehenge.

Bobby looked pleased and supportive when she told him, but inwardly his heart sank to his shoes. How could Tina travel with him and the team with a baby? How could they afford it? What if she had to quit work? What if his time with the majors was short-lived? Or what if his time with the majors, and his travels, went on and on and on....

Tina was just as conflicted. She'd never been one of those girls who babysat or longed for her own children. She wanted kids (someday), but not until she'd risen in her career. One day at work she confided in a new friend, someone with whom she'd clicked the first time they worked on an assignment together. Her friend was climbing the ladder, too, and hadn't let an unwanted pregnancy derail her agenda. She talked to Tina about an abortion. Tina was embarrassed that it sounded so good. She didn't like the idea of abortions but, after all, it was her body and her life. Wasn't that what everyone was saying? She wasn't ready to be saddled with children yet. What a waste of her education and abilities!

That night she made a knockout dinner for Bobby. She took the phone off the hook, lit a few candles, and turned on a smooth jazz CD. Bobby came in to dinner, raised his eyebrows at the spread but *didn't question anything, so as not to pop the dream bubble. After dinner over cappuccinos from their new machine, Tina told him she wanted an abortion. As she was explaining her reasoning, several of the candles burned out and the CD finished playing.*

Bobby didn't know what to say. Sure, the baby was a complication, but already he was beginning to like the idea. Then again, it would be easier to begin a family in a year or so. But abortion? It would take him awhile to process all this and rethink the plan. But he was part of a small men's Bible study now, and they'd been talking about how to approach some of the stickier ethical decisions confronting couples nowadays. The guys had been learning how to evaluate their decisions using the Bible as a measuring stick. He had a pretty strong sense that this decision had a clear right and wrong about it.

Helping Tina clear the table, he offered to do the dishes. He actually put them in the dishwasher this time rather than just rinsing them and stacking them in the sink. Tina was impressed. Then he sat her down at the kitchen counter and began trying to explain to her what he was learning in his Bible study. She wasn't impressed anymore. It was their first big fight.

For several days they barely spoke. Tina was mad. Bobby was hurt. Tina felt trapped; Bobby felt powerless.

The Body of Christ

Imagine a time when the church is once again the bastion of healthy cultural mores, when it becomes, as it should, the place we go to for direction and answers in those difficult passages of life. Imagine a time when evangelism and discipleship are co-priorities with the social aspects of the gospel. Imagine a time when the body of Christ works like one organism, where every part is healthy and performing at its peak. Imagine a time when society takes on the face of the church rather than the other way around. Imagine a time when the body of Christ is known by its love—by what it's *for* instead of what it's *against*. Imagine a time when the body of Christ actually glows in the dark places of the world.

If churches are ever to be counted among the radiant cities on the hill that Jesus spoke of, if they are going to grow to define the culture rather than reflect it for couples like Bobby and Tina, we have some changes to make. We have new priorities to set, priorities that require us to focus on the big picture, the actual war, rather than the petty battles Satan uses to divide...and conquer...us. He endeavors to blind us to the impact we can have if we fight together. He wants us caught up in extremism, selfishness, denominationalism, legalism, and anything that separates us.

But God revels in the diversity of His people. He's placed us in communities, neighborhoods, and cultures that reflect many different strengths and needs. He's neither surprised nor discouraged by our different expressions of faith. But He does want us to come together around the basic tenets of the gospel, grow as believers, and be available as His ambassadors within our communities and outside of them.

So let's take a look at the body of Christ, the church.

First, a definition: the body of Christ is the church. The church is any gathering of God-believing people who agree that He loved the world enough to send His Son Jesus to pay the penalty for our sin, and who rest in the grace of that gift as their means of salvation. Throughout the world there are mega-churches, small local churches, denomination-affiliated churches, house churches. There are churches built upon doctrine, upon social issues, and upon mutual needs. There are churches on the windswept tundra, in the jungle, the bush, the desert, downtown, on campus, in the suburbs, and now on the Internet. A gathering of believers is a church regardless of location and external description.

In recent days, the church has been moving ever closer to the first-century model. The early church met in homes as small groups, probably gathering in larger assemblies for the Jewish holidays. Americans are coming to realize the difference between the local "celebration" (everyone together on Sunday mornings) and the subcongregations or "cells," small groups put together along all sorts of affinity lines. The strongest, healthiest churches are those with both celebrations and cells. A cell is the place where the greatest spiritual work is done.

One of the outstanding churches in the world is Kampala Pentecostal Church in the capital of Uganda, pastored by Canadian Gary Skinner. Gary has set it up so that the vast majority of his twelve thousand members are in small groups directed by one leader and one leader in training. They always have multiplication in mind. Once the cell has grown to eight members, it divides into another group with another leader and leader in training. They become family for one another, so important in AIDS-ravaged Africa.

Such connection and accountability are equally important in affluent America, where our independence shields us from our need to grow as believers. *Interdependence* is essential if we are going to build a healthy church.

What Are Our Priorities?

The ultimate goal of the church is to glorify God and to present Jesus as the "author and finisher of our faith" (Hebrews 12:2, NKJV). In John 17:20–21, Jesus said our most effective proof of the gospel is the radical love of the body of Christ for one another.

It's unity.

He said to the Father, "My prayer is not for them alone. I pray also for those who will believe in me through their message, that all of them may be one, Father, just as you are in me and I am in you. May they also be in us *so that the world may believe that you have sent me*" (vv. 20–21, NIV, emphasis ours).

Jesus wasn't talking about union, where everyone's in the same place. You can be in the same home or the same church and not have unity. He wasn't talking about uniformity, where everyone looks alike. Unity is not unanimity, where everyone agrees. There will always be a need and a place for great debate and discussion and the energizing dynamics of personality.

Unity is a spirit of oneness, and it's so unusual and attractive it stops people right in their tracks. It's one thing for us individually to love God; it's another for a group of people to love God by radically loving one another. People are compelled to Christ if we love one another in a sacrificial, no-holds-barred way. This is what Francis Schaeffer called the "ultimate apologetic." This is what attracts people. It is the proof of the gospel.

We see it worked out in the book of Acts where believers were caught up in loving God and loving each other, meeting physical, emotional, and spiritual needs, and finding that in giving themselves away they received more than they imagined.

Deep in our heart of hearts, we know this is the true definition of the church. Yet every now and then, we require a perspective check.

Some years ago I (Ron) came to some interesting conclusions regarding the state of the church when I traveled the country in a motor home with my wife and another couple doing research for my doctorate. After interviewing 300 prominent Christian leaders in 175 churches in 38 states, I concluded that in many instances there appeared to be a great zeal for God's *work,* but without a corresponding passion for *God Himself.*

As we traveled, we observed that many Christian leaders, the most influential people in the church, were drifting subtly into a powerless, lifeless existence. There was form but little substance. There was Christian acting but not Christian living. The power and love and joy of intimacy with Christ, which we expected to see in these leaders, did not seem to characterize them. We took it as a warning for our own lives. (Interestingly, the most brilliant exception was our meeting at Arrowhead Springs with Bill, who spoke, with tears running down his cheeks, of his love for Jesus.)

Loving God, loving people. That's our job. The results are God's to give.

We also recognized in our research the tendency to relegate the "work of the ministry" to the "ministry professionals," the pastors, teachers, and ministry leaders. But that is not the intent of God. We are *all* to be about ministry; we are *all* to be loving God and loving people.

"What Can I Give?"

God has called us to live our lives totally dependent on Him. He is the one who calls every one of us to minister, and we need to live in obedience to Him by the power of the Holy Spirit. Such lives will be an example to those who follow us. We need to be people of prayer, letting it shape and direct every facet of our lives—relationships, work, play, time, and money. We need to be evangelists and disciplers, recognizing that while not all have the gift of evangelism, all *are* called to be part of God's mission to draw people to Himself. We can't refuse the mandate by claiming, "That's not my gift." We should be devoted to studying God's Word for the purpose of obeying what He has commanded us to do in every area of life, including our politics, education, finances, and citizenship. And all that we do should be characterized by love for God and each other.

Intimacy with God and personal holiness must once again become central in the life of the church, at every level. We can't emphasize this enough. We Christians have been repeatedly—and far too often deservedly—criticized for our lack of sincerity and our hypocrisy. If there's anything that will cure us of insincerity, it's getting to know the God who gives His life for others. And if there's anything that will cure us of our two-facedness, it's the life of holistic and holy integrity (where we're the same in public as in private) that flows out of this life. Inward renewal can't help but bleed out into cultural transformation, especially when thirsty men and women see it in the church!

One of God's laws says that he who seeks happiness never finds it, but he who lives to help and serve others finds true fulfillment and meaning in life.

We are conditioned in North America to view such institutions as the church with the jaundiced eye of the consumer. We search from church to church for the best worship team, the best communicator, the most pleasing facility—the one with the basketball court or the well-stocked bookstore. Somehow along the way we've lost the point that when we gather with believers our motivation is to give, rather than get.

We should be meeting together to give praise to God

through worship and prayer, listening to sermons and teaching not as critics, but as sponges, soaking up what God has to say through His servants *so that* "the body of Christ may be built up," as it says in Ephesians 4:12 (NIV). It's the "one-anothers" again—support one another, encourage one another, build one another up, pray for one another. The churches that work like a body works, each part doing what it is created to do, have the healthiest members.

That means we have to change our way of relating to the church. We have to be alert to opportunities to be used—as teachers, as bulletin stuffers, as greeters, as mentors, as servants. We have to sign up for areas that need volunteers, join worship teams, go to Bible studies, show up at picnics and baptisms, go on mission trips, hold babies, take our neighbors to Christmas programs, enroll our kids in Sunday school and youth groups, and pray for our pastors, teachers, counselors, and musicians. We have to step out of our comfort zones and look for ways to serve.

And we really don't have any time to lose! Every day our compassionate Lord will open up opportunities to touch broken, hurting lives in His name. But we have to open our eyes.

"Should I Know Her?"

A pastor's wife shared with us a conversation that forever changed the way she looks at ministry. A friend came up to her one Sunday and asked if she knew a particular woman. Cheryl tried to place the name but couldn't, and asked, "*Should* I know her?"

"I thought you would," answered her friend wistfully. "She lives three doors down from you, and she's dying of cancer." Cheryl didn't know what to say. She'd been too busy to notice…and her neighbor died three days later.

That conversation was instrumental in developing Cheryl and her husband's conviction to ease up on the church-sponsored activities that threatened to take up every weeknight, and to wake up their congregation to the needs around them.

Surely one of Satan's most divisive ploys is extremism and isolationism. He wants us too busy to go where God *really* wants us, and too absorbed in our pet convictions to see the whole plan of God. Some churches and denominations can focus so heavily on Bible teaching, evangelism, and discipleship that they ignore the social aspects of the gospel, while others focus so much on "doing the work of the ministry" that they stray from the truth and study of the Word and the importance of salvation.

But evangelism, discipleship, and social involvement are *all* essential; in fact, they go together. There are numerous opportunities for churches to be involved in social causes while at the same time furthering the goals of evangelism and discipleship. Churches are where the world goes when there's trouble or hardship or need for protection, spiritual or otherwise.

The Other Side of the "Burn"

There's a church that really blends the Word and the work in St. Andrews, Scotland. The birthplace of golf. A vacation destination known for its beautiful shoreline, breathtaking ruins, and quaint small-town feel. Not the kind of place we think of as the front lines of battle.

Yet a few years ago St. Andrews Baptist Church noticed that all the town's churches were concentrated along a golden corridor within the town proper—but most of those who actually make their home in St. Andrews live on the other side of the burn (Scots for "river"), and are often reluctant to go to the more cosmopolitan, upper-class section of town.

So the Baptists did what missions groups have been calling believers worldwide to do more recently—instead of waiting for "them" to come to "us," the church went to "them." They moved their Sunday morning service out to the local high school, Madras College, right in the middle of the neighborhoods they were trying to reach and transform for Christ.

Presence was a major step, but more needed to be done. Some church members began researching the needs of the town, particularly the four primary (elementary) schools, and developed a systematic plan for offering practical help to struggling families. "Families First-St. Andrews" started with a staff of one, plus a whole load of volunteers. While they had a clear sense of mission and knew the boundaries of a well-articulated plan, they also grew in the direction of the needs that arose.

Sometimes it was simply recognizing the stress of a single mom who needed someone to talk to or do a little babysitting. Other times it was addressing abusive situations in which local social work might be involved. Families First was there throughout the process to support the family and make sure no one fell through the cracks. Then again, it might be stopping by homes of lonely elderly people who just needed a weekly visitor who cared and some help with local errands. In mornings and afternoons, it was breakfast or snacks coupled with games, art, and sports for kids whose parents needed some help. It is an unstoppably glowing fellowship.

If you were to go to St. Andrews Baptist Church this next Sunday, there's a good chance you'd see a bunch of kids sitting along the front row. Tough kids with tough lives. But kids who are growing in the knowledge that they are loved by God and His people. A tough process, too, with lots of mistakes, but one in which people and a town see themselves moving from the kingdom of darkness to the kingdom of light.

The Bigger Picture

The church is at its most glorious in the midst of distress and persecution, when the superficial things are put aside for survival. In the persecuted church around the globe believers are at once vulnerable and virile. They are targets in a dark world, yet the battle lines are clear and their spiritual armor protects them.

In the West, "attacks" on believers come in the form of

busyness, materialism, criticism, ingratitude, conformity. We categorize these attacks as distractions, minimizing their effectiveness in robbing us of the joys in serving God and loving people. That's just where Satan wants us—"filled and unfulfilled," as Henri Nouwen says. Oh, that we would open our eyes to the bigger picture of the worldwide body of Christ, accept our petty struggles for what they are, and join the fight against darkness.

The church needs to penetrate the influence centers of its communities.

A rural community church in Oregon has added a citizenship class to its adult Sunday school schedule. A Southern Baptist church in suburban San Diego provides homework centers in a nearby working-class neighborhood. A mainline denominational church in Maryland works with some of the top political and media leaders in Washington, D.C. Thousands and thousands of Christian teenagers—the young body of Christ!—meet at their schools' flagpoles every September to pray for their friends, their schools, and the upcoming academic year.

In our Western oversensitivity to not impose our faith on anyone, we are in danger of hiding this truth "under a basket," as Jesus said in Matthew 5:15. It makes no sense to keep the reason for our joy a secret! Make no mistake. Everyone lives in light of some kind of belief system, and whatever we believe permeates our activity. Those who assert the importance of separating one's faith in God from one's public life, or workplace, or school, don't realize or acknowledge that we all live out what we believe to some extent. To *not* live that way would produce a life-robbing tension none of us could live under for long. (And could that be the source of "stress" that physicians repeatedly warn will shorten our lives?)

We must *believe* and *demonstrate* that the Bible and the body of Christ are relevant to life in the twenty-first century. Churches are poised to show that relevance if they are not afraid. But that's where Satan gets us. It's a prime battle-ground.

Precautious or Prevailing?

Our friend and longtime pastor, Randy Pope, distinguishes between two types of churches—a prevailing church and a precautious church.

The dictionary defines prevailing as "gaining the advantage or mastery, being victorious, effective, stronger." Randy writes that a prevailing church "is a place where the presence of God's power is demonstrated with such force that the community in which it exists is marked with an indelible spiritual imprint."

On the other hand, there is the precautious church. Webster's defines precautious as "taking necessary measure against possible danger, harm or failure." Randy points out that the "precautious church is free from failure only because of its unwillingness to attempt great accomplishments for the sake of God and His Kingdom."[14]

To Randy, pastor of a prevailing church in Atlanta, "precautious" is not an option. He looks for any and every possible way that his church can make inroads into the community. His congregation goes where the people are, strikes up conversations and relationships, and woos seekers into the body of Christ.

Randy has identified as part of his personal mission field the local golf and tennis clubs. He and others he's enlisted and trained play their rounds and their matches, and then hold discussions over lunch for club members on such topics as "Why do bad things happen to good people?" and "How do you explain evil in our world?"

In the context of the discussion Randy brings in the Bible as a reference point. In a nonthreatening way, Randy and his team influence senior level executives, who have a genuine curiosity. Many have come to Christ in the process and have found a home in Randy's church.

Pastor Rick Warren's book *The Purpose-Driven Church* further describes the healthy twenty-first century church as one that is willing to risk and fail. But when it fails, it fails *forward,* learning, growing, adjusting all the time, but without compromise.

It's not too big of a goal to expect God to use us in the communities in which He's placed us! Is our faith big enough to believe that we could be the change agent in a community? Can we believe Him to give us openings to minister and then to equip us to be His lights? Can we believe Him to stir us up enough to move us out of our comfort zones?

In 1899, Theodore Roosevelt said, "Far better to dare mighty things, to win glorious triumphs, even though checkered by failure, than to take rank with those poor spirits who neither enjoy much, nor suffer much, because they live in the grey twilight that knows no victory, nor defeat."

Roosevelt was not talking about churches, per se, nor specifically to the body of Christ in this statement. But the sentiment could be read as a depiction of the first-century church and the giants of faith throughout the history of Christianity. And it can be read as a not-so-gentle admonition to those of us tempted to read about glowing in the dark, but choosing to roll over and go back to sleep instead.

There is no limit to the potential of the church when it creatively helps God's people reach their maximum effectiveness in the war against Satan's kingdom. Without this commitment on the part of the local churches in each city, the battle will not be won. *The church must once again be the church!*

An ever darker, sometimes despairing world needs to see a city on a hill with all lights blazing.

VIEW OF THE KINGDOM OF DARKNESS	VIEW OF THE KINGDOM OF LIGHT
The church is a repressive anachronism today.	The church is a place of vitality and health.
Love of self is primary.	Love of God and neighbor is central.
The church is inconsequential to the real world.	The church is salt and light in the middle of this generation.
The professionals are the only ones who minister.	All believers are ministers.
The church is a single-focus ministry.	The church does evangelism, discipleship, and cares for the needs of the community.
Independence reigns.	Interdependence, support, and accountability are central.
The separation of church and state excludes any role in society.	The church is a foundational institution in society.

ACTION STEPS

▸ Take some time to meditate on Ephesians 4:11–16.

▸ When you encounter the phrase "for the equipping of
the saints for the work of service," how do you react?
Do you believe you are in ministry yourself? In fact,
how do you respond to this statement, "We're all in full-
time ministry; it's just a matter of where we get our
paycheck"? Take a few minutes right now and process
your thoughts on that, perhaps with a friend. What are
the implications?

▸ Find a recent copy of your church's bulletin, or go
online to examine its priorities. Taking into account
your abilities, your schedule, and what you sense God is
calling you to do, how can you get involved in what
your church is doing?

▸ Write out three very specific prayer points for the
leadership of your church, or connect with an already-
established prayer ministry. Establish a specific, weekly
time to pray for pastors, teachers, Sunday school
teachers, and worship leaders.

5

Hide It Under a Bushel?

Impacting the Marketplace

▶▶ *There was no mistaking the war Andy was fighting. There was nothing subtle about it—every day his wife, his kids, and his boss wanted something from him. He had long ago given up any thought of balance—or rather, that's all he was doing, running around like a clown trying to keep all the balls in the air.*

He didn't regret those balls. They were what he'd chosen—a wife with spirit and charm, two girls who took his breath away when he saw them all dressed up, a son who was just coming into his own with a soccer ball, and a good job in a development company with

men and women he enjoyed. But there was still a war out there—
for his time, his resources, and his heart.

Those were some of his thoughts that Thursday morning when
he drove to work in Southern California. He certainly had a lot of
time to think. That was the one and only good thing to say about
gridlock. He was stuck in the second lane behind a black pickup
with naked woman mud flaps that waved at him when the speed
of the traffic picked up a bit, which wasn't very often. "Jeff & Jer"
were on the radio, dispensing their constant chatter and weighing
in on the trivial issues of the day. The cars in the carpool lane sped
by and Andy just knew the occupants were smirking at his next-
to-nothing progress.

He couldn't quite put his finger on this "winter of his discontent." He was generally a happy guy. It wasn't the insane
commute. It wasn't the inane radio commentary. It wasn't his job
or the other circumstances of his life. He had everything he set out
for. If some angel tapped him on the shoulder and said, "I'll give
you whatever you wish," he wouldn't be able to think of a thing. Yet
he was in the grip of a strange malaise, a restlessness, that he could
tell might take him down if he wasn't careful. And he was a little
tired of being careful.

Andy found a parking spot not too far away from the job site,
and picked his way across the muddy lot to the trailer where his
foreman stood. He was thinking he should have worn his work
boots even though his site visit would be short, when his cell phone
rang. It was his boss checking in. He answered the phone cheer-
fully, but as he talked, multitasking with a work order on the
clipboard, he found himself distracted and irritated by his fore-

man's illegible handwriting and the pinup calendar on the wall. Amazing how one could communicate cheerfulness over the phone with a snarl on his lips.

At his office, he put on his company smile, shook all the hands he passed, and shoved all thoughts of discontent into the recesses of his mind. All day long he mindlessly filled any idle moment with some sort of activity, even resorting to setting up the portable putting green he kept rolled up under his desk. When the memo came through that he was slated to join the management team at a training session the next day, he barely let it register. He drove home with the traffic again, singing along with Peggy Lee, "Is That All There Is?"

Friday morning, Andy joined his co-workers, even a few he didn't know very well, in the conference room overlooking the koi pond by the entrance to the building. Two "outsiders" joined them, a slim, dark-haired man with close-set eyes and an older blond guy with the rosy cheeks of a golfer. They corralled the group and began a daylong session the likes of which Andy had never experienced.

The two facilitators, one a marriage and family counselor and the other an expert in life management and coaching, began by taking the team through exercises that Andy squirmed under…until at the morning break he noticed that he finally knew the last names of each of his team members and a little bit about their lives. Andy and the team were challenged to examine their ethics and integrity, both words that had been floating around the business journals but neither of which had ever been discussed in his presence.

For the first time in his twenty-two years of work experience, someone addressed the idea that the work environment was a place to serve others, to live out your belief system. That a greater purpose than meeting quotas or building buildings is how you do it—how you treat your co-workers, how you treat your clients, your level of honesty, whether you overcharge, overbook, or oversell.

After lunch, the team discussed stress management and conflict resolution. Andy considered himself a pretty easy guy to get along with until, in this relatively safe environment, his assistant mentioned how short tempered he had been the last six months. He thought he dealt with conflicts well, until his secretary shyly reminded him that one of his clients was still so mad at him they couldn't collect the rest of his payment. By the end of the day, Andy's team, well managed even if they weren't adept at dealing with some of the issues brought up that day, dispersed with several action steps and a time frame in which to accomplish them. They included Andy's actually apologizing to his disgruntled client, a thorough assessment of inventory procedures, and a company-wide strategy to put the concepts of ethics and integrity before all employees.

Andy left work that day with his head spinning. He'd taken a good look at himself and his responsibilities in his company and, while it was a little convicting, it had given him a new determination and a new set of objectives to shoot for. He finally had a new sense of purpose and direction for his life. He walked to his car with a lighter step than he'd had for months. He called Carol and convinced her to get a sitter and to be ready to go out for a long dinner where he could tell her all he'd learned that day. He couldn't wait.

The Marketplace Christian

How does our faith relate to business? In the late 1970s a handful of businessmen in Atlanta got together to examine that very question. They took the phrase "What would Jesus do?" from Charles Sheldon's hundred-year-old masterpiece *In His Steps* and used it as the jumping-off place for a new organization of privately owned companies whose owners/CEOs wanted to do a better job of integrating their faith with their businesses. Originally called Fellowship of Companies for Christ International and recently renamed Christ@Work[15], their vision statement is "Transforming our world through Christ...one company leader at a time."

In an interview, Bruce Wilkinson, founder and former president of Walk Through the Bible, one of Christ@Work's first conference speakers and a member of their board of directors, explained the focus:

> A Christian company isn't necessarily better than a non-Christian company, but it should be different in its purpose. The members of FCCI are committed to using their businesses as a platform for ministry. We have three goals in addition to making a profit: One is the salvation of our employees as well as others in our sphere of influence; two, the spiritual growth of these people; and three, service to our community. We try to get members to take part of their tithe, part of their time, and some of their company profits to help accomplish these goals.[16]

Periodically Christ@Work sponsors conferences in which speakers teach biblical principles on finances, leadership, goal setting, and management. "Most Christian businessmen have lost the idea that our work is our platform for ministry," says Wilkinson. "Often the ones who are known for their verbal testimony stand out negatively. They may pay their employees poorly, or simply run a poor shop. Christianity should include excellence in business as well as a verbal witness."

So why is this so often *not* the case? Ed Silvoso, president of Harvest Evangelism, suggests one reason: "The most common self-inflicted put-down is, 'I am not a pastor—I am just a layperson.' This is all part of a clever satanic scheme to neutralize apostles, prophets, evangelists, pastors, and teachers along with the entire army of disciples, already positioned in the marketplace."[17]

Fortune magazine calls people who mix God and business "rebels on several fronts. They reject the centuries-old American conviction that spirituality is a private matter. They challenge religious thinkers who disdain business as an inherently impure pursuit. They disagree with business people who say that religion is unavoidably divisive."[18] Businessmen and women who follow Jesus Christ are breaking all kinds of barriers.

There's a real revolution going on in the marketplace today! In fact, we believe we're going through a second reformation. Prior to Luther's storied revolt in 1517, the word of God was the "property" of the church, which interpreted and applied it to the people. No layperson could read and study the Bible on his own.

The first reformation freed up the *Word of God* for the common person, the layman. Yet the *work of God*, which the New Testament church understood as part of our responsibility as the "priesthood of believers," remained the activity of the professional clergy. This current reformation is opening the work of God to the average person. And business leaders are finding in this work the answer to their need for meaning in life.

Bob Briner, author of *Roaring Lambs*, maintained that significance comes when we join the bandwagon to penetrate our culture as salt and light. Yes, there are appropriate and inappropriate ways to do this. Yes, there are legal matters to which we must be sensitive. But let us not, in fear, refuse to be used by God. We must model His principles, elevate His truths, and be the best employers/employees we can be.[19]

Does God have something to say to the majority of us who hold secular jobs? Os Hillman says, "Well, consider that 122 of Jesus' 132 public appearances in the New Testament were in the marketplace. And of the 52 parables Jesus told, 45 had a workplace context. Finally, would you believe that 39 of the 40 divine interventions recorded in Acts took place in the marketplace? Not in church. At work."[20]

How Do We Glow in the Dark at Work?

So, practically speaking, how do we do it? How do we allow the radiance and hope of our union with the Lord Jesus

Christ to penetrate the corridors and cubicles, the shops and warehouses of today's marketplace?

Employers, give generously and joyously to your employees.

There seems to be a growing trend in business that we like very much! We're hearing reports from different segments of the marketplace about family-friendly businesses with flextime that takes into account workers' varied schedules. Benefits such as on-site childcare, fitness centers, and employee-owned businesses have been edging their way into enlightened areas of the working world. This reflects years of union intervention and worker demands, but it also reflects a healthy trend, recognizing the inherent value of everyone from the top down.

But let's take it a step further. As in the fictional story that opens this chapter, one of my colleagues and I (Ron) meet regularly with the management team of a large technology company. Our job is to help them become a *better* team. We begin with exercises that get them quickly talking about issues in their lives that affect their outlook on life and work. We get them to examine their methods of dealing with conflict, we talk about trust and forgiveness, and we prompt them to evaluate their stress levels and devise ways to deal with it.

After one long day we went around the circle and I asked each man (though we often have women in our groups) what one thing he could do by year-end that would mean success to him.

The very first guy said he would call it success if he could have just one good night's sleep. I asked him to elaborate. He said he was so worried about the success of the company that he hadn't slept well in months. The rest of the team was visibly moved by his admission...and the previously impenetrable walls began to crumble. The next guy said by the end of the year he hoped to reconcile with his wife who had just divorced him. One man said he intended to get back to regular church attendance with his family. The depth of transparency and feeling was something they'd never experienced before as a team.

The Christian CEO of this company has made the decision to put a significant chunk of his human resource budget into a program that introduces biblically consistent values to his people. He knows that we will not violate his trust by offending his employees or insisting on conversions, but that we will present time-honored, consistent truth and show its application to the work world. And that we will share our faith when asked.

By the time our contract ends, this CEO's employees will have learned ways of relating to each other that will significantly increase their productivity, build up their families, and strengthen their character. And they will have worked long enough with a couple of normal Christian guys that they will not be afraid to pursue spiritual conversations in the future should they so choose.

Employers, your greatest asset is your employees. It's been proven that happy employees make for better bottom lines. But again, let's go a step further. As believers, we ought to lead the charge in people development. Frankly, we don't have a choice. We live in a dysfunctional culture. We have to reparent our culture, in a very real sense. We have to help those entering the work force today, many of whom grew up in dysfunctional homes, learn how to develop strong "emotional quotients," Daniel Goleman's term for personal and interpersonal skills.

The book of Proverbs is full of "emotional quotient" skills that address self-awareness, resolving conflict, relating to people, dealing with strengths and weaknesses, and life balance. All these are essential skills that seem to be missing in the character of many young adults.[21]

Especially lacking today is a commitment to absolute truth and values aligned with it. Once again, Socrates' comment about straight and crooked lines applies. One of our jobs is to help young men and women, and everyone around us for that matter, develop those straight lines, from the CEO to the parking attendant.

In a very real sense, this is preevangelism. As we are salt and light in the culture—vulnerable, relational, interesting, caring—we give people many opportunities to grapple with these principles and the power behind them. It's part of the process. Particularly in this postmodern age, when people are turning away from absolutes, there is a desperate need for such strategies.

Looking after our employees does not mean that we over-look poor work, but it does change our approach. Because we believe that people are created in the image of God, we treat them with respect and kindness. We, above all others, are to reflect Christ's love and compassion. It is a love that finds expression in the second great commandment, "Love your neighbor as yourself" (Matthew 22:39), and the Golden Rule, "Do to others what you would have them do to you" (Matthew 7:12, NIV).

Therefore, when we have to let people go, we do it with dignity, with assistance when applicable, and in many cases with the attitude of encouraging them to find a job better suited to their talents. "Do nothing from selfishness or empty conceit," Paul says in Philippians 2:3–4, "but with humility of mind regard one another as more important than yourselves; do not merely look out for your own personal interests, but also for the interests of others."

John Couch, vice president of education for Apple Computer, tells of his experiences in the early days of the company. He ascribes the company's meteoric growth, in great part, to the prevailing mind-set of the leadership concerning the importance of people.

Once, one of his associates went through a tragic divorce and slipped into a dark depression. John learned that each night his friend drove forty minutes home to his empty house, and that the memories there were devastating to him.

So John quietly rented an apartment close to the office for his friend and employee so he wouldn't have such a long drive and such negatively reinforced memories. He provided this as a bonus for the man. In addition, various staff invited him over regularly for meals to ease the pain of transition.

That is generosity and devotion; that is love in action. And that ought to typify a Christian's business lifestyle.

Employees, give generously and joyously to your employers.

In the same breath that we talk about *employers* giving to their workers, we want to remind *employees* of their opportunities to glow in the dark. We all know people who cut corners at work. In fact, it has become a cultural joke to cast the boss as the bad guy and take what you can from him.

That sort of attitude, of course, is 180 degrees from the heart of God for His children.

Do you use too much work time to take care of personal matters? Do you allow yourself to get caught up in office gossip or in joking around in a way that might make you blush in another setting? Are you conscious of doing your absolute best to fulfill your work obligations? Ephesians 6:7 says, "Serve wholeheartedly, as if you were serving the Lord, not men" (NIV).

Heeding such a simple admonition—or ignoring it—can make or break our witness at work. Regardless of our positions, our salaries, or our hours, *we* can change lives by the way we approach our jobs. We can choose to speak kindly and respectfully, we can choose to be on time and work our hardest, we can choose to support those above us.

Have you considered adding your employer and your co-workers to your prayer list? Somehow, God takes our kindnesses and our prayers and not only uses them in the lives of others, but also adds them up and one day will reward us for them.

If we lived according to Philippians 2 in an office environment, what would that look like? It might mean choosing the least attractive desk—the one no one wants. Then again, it might involve volunteering to do a menial task that someone has to do but everyone avoids—making the coffee in the morning, maybe? Cleaning the bathrooms every week? Word has it that Mother Teresa used to take the last pair of shoes donated to the Sisters of Charity. At the end of her life, her feet were in chronic pain as a result of wearing shoes that didn't fit her. Little shoes, big soul.

Graciously serve your customers.
ServiceMaster offers a range of services (plant management, housekeeping, laundry, food services) for health care, educational, residential, and industrial clients. Founded in 1929 by a former minor league baseball player as a moth-proofing company, it has grown to encompass twelve familiar home-service brands like Terminix, Rescue Rooter, and TruGreen ChemLawn. Its founder, Marion E. Wade, was a man of faith. He and his successors established ServiceMaster's four objectives: To honor God in all we do; to help people develop; to pursue excellence; and to grow profitably.[22]

In the core of its business philosophy, ServiceMaster has created a hierarchy of values consistently placed before its employees and customers. It covers the gamut. Profit is not ignored but is a reasonable expectation when God and people are honored and excellence is built into the vision. As Chuck Stair, a former group president of the company, explained, "The first two goals are the end goals; the last two are the means. We work joyfully and very hard to serve people."[23]

Or take an example from the beleaguered airline industry—JetBlue. In the midst of the near collapse of the air travel industry, JetBlue has emerged out of nowhere and, amazingly, turned a profit. CEO David Neeleman takes a pragmatic approach with the company, and he also knows how to serve JetBlue's customers. In addition to "scratching where they itch" by providing leather seats and satellite TV, he's out to try "a little harder than the other lines to treat our customers well."

Neeleman says: "I think people see passengers as an annoyance...We realize that they pay our way every day." All well and good, but does it make any difference? One snapshot tells a lot: *everyone*, including the CEO (who flies once a week—just to keep up-to-date) and the pilots, pick up trash at the end of each flight. It's about building a posture of continual giving, and JetBlue is doing it.[24]

When Jesus was being questioned one day by His disciples, who were jockeying for positions of authority in His kingdom, He responded:

"You know that the rulers of the Gentiles lord it over them, and their great men exercise authority over them. It is not this way among you, but whoever wishes to become great among you shall be your servant, and whoever wishes to be first among you shall be your slave; just as the Son of Man did not come to be served, but to serve, and to give His life a ransom for many." (Matthew 20:25–28)

Clearly, in business this means Christians should service the customer in every way possible. Obviously, we should provide the product or service we offer in an excellent way. Less obvious is the way we can serve our customers spiritually. We can pray for them, ask about any needs, listen to them, and even, in appropriate settings, give them our testimonies and the gospel.

In-N-Out Burger[25] began in 1948 as California's very first drive-through hamburger stand. Harry and Esther Snyder's business philosophy holds to this day: "Give customers the freshest, highest quality foods you can buy and provide them with friendly service in a sparkling clean environment."

While other "hamburger stands" and franchises report losses, In-N-Out is stronger than ever. They still steer clear of freezers, microwaves, and heat lamps. They unload fresh vine-ripe tomatoes every other day and cut them by hand. Their beef is additive free and ground in their own facility. Every hamburger is made fresh when it's ordered. French fries are cut in the store, one potato at a time as needed.

But this company goes a step further. Paper beverage cups and French fry and burger bags are printed with a Bible reference, quiet testimony to the Snyders' faith: John 3:16; Revelation 3:20; Proverbs 3:5. Also, In-N-Out has created a foundation that assists abused children. According to the website, the company pays *all* costs associated with running the foundation and distributing the funds. Therefore, 100 percent of donations go directly to the children.

God has given all of us positions of influence.

Conduct all your business with integrity.
It is often said that you cannot be successful in business unless you cheat someone, produce an inferior product, pay less than fair wages, or manipulate crooked deals.

In fact, the contrary is true.

Long-range success depends upon reliability, integrity, authenticity, honesty, and priority consideration for employees and customers alike.

A friend of ours, currently serving as a high-ranking professional in the Pentagon, defines biblical integrity in the workplace this way: "To me it wears the face of honesty, fairness, and consistency in one's dealings. I try to be open and direct. That doesn't mean folks will agree with what I'm saying, but they can get an honest answer. I don't think biblical integrity means trying to make people happy all the time. That's diplomacy. Sometimes standing up for what is right will draw criticism and make people unhappy. To lead, you must be prepared for criticism. Jesus certainly drew a lot of criticism."

Beware of becoming calloused or greedy.
Businesses are rightly concerned to make a profit. Money is certainly not a bad thing, and we believe the Lord wants to financially bless companies that honor Him in the way they do business.

But a word of caution is in order here. Paul warned his young disciple Timothy of the danger of loving money. He wrote, "Those who want to get rich fall into temptation and a snare and many foolish and harmful desires which plunge men into ruin and destruction. For the love of money is a root of all sorts of evil, and some by longing for it have wandered away from the faith and pierced themselves with many griefs" (1 Timothy 6:9–10).

We believe that a free enterprise system allows for more personal freedom than other economic systems. Not only is there greater freedom to be responsible and demonstrate charitable love, but there is also the freedom to be irresponsible, dishonest, and greedy. The inherent weakness is not in this economic system but in the nature of man.

We must wear the cloak of materialism loosely. Further, we must be careful that we do not view our salvation as grounded in, or exemplified by, our economic system. Instead, we should view every area of life, including our economic system, as an opportunity to demonstrate responsible stewardship, quality work, honesty, and charity before God, who owns all things.

Money is merely a medium of exchange. But the insatiable desire for more and more money is dangerous. If we follow the tendency to trust riches rather than God, we fail to acknowledge the real Source from whom all blessings come. No matter how much God blesses us, it all belongs to Him, and we are His stewards. All of us will reach a point when we are tempted to allow money (or the things we use our money to buy) to compete with the Lord for our affections.

My (Ron) son Matt will never forget when his friend Anne led a Bible study on the passage where Jesus says, "where your treasure is, your heart will be also." At the end of the study, Anne reflected, "I think I've been loving my CDs too much recently, so here they are…please take whatever you want."

Paul, in Ephesians 4:28, gives us the reason for increasing our riches through our labors. "But rather he must labor, performing with his own hands what is good, *so that he will have something to share* with one who has need." God wants us to be His wealth distributors. Blessing comes from giving, not getting.

We are not, then, to work in order to have a flashier standard of living. This doesn't mean that anyone with two cars is disobeying the Lord. But it does mean that our pleasure is not to be what drives our work. We're to work in order to help others. "Blessed to be a blessing" is how God describes it in his covenant with Abraham.

If this is our perspective, it wouldn't seem right to try and shove the other guy out of the way in jockeying for a promotion. We also might think twice before spending our extra cash on another toy or gadget. Maybe we'd buy a gift for a loved one or friend or send an anonymous envelope with cash in it to a co-worker in need.

If we're blessed to be a blessing and have been given extra time (maybe we're single, or maybe the kids are grown and we're retired, or maybe we just have Thursday nights free), how would we spend it? Hopefully not in more TV. Is there a co-worker we can build a relationship with, particularly someone who might be hurting or lonely? Can we go do some decorating or gardening or cleaning at an elderly person's house? Can we volunteer to babysit for stressed-out friends or teach computer skills to a nontechie? None of this means that we never do anything fun or anything that we like to do. It just means that our priorities are recalibrated such that others come first.

A Word for the Rest of Us...

Plenty of adults these days do not consider themselves as "in the marketplace." We're self-employed, working out of our garage; we're moms with carpools and PTA; we're students finishing degrees and wondering where we'll end up; we're missionaries in foreign cultures; we're retired, spending more time with our grandkids than co-workers. Yet the marketplace is all around us and a place with which we interact pretty much every day. In fact, because we're not tied down to one work environment, we may have *more* opportunities to spread a little light.

Everyplace we go we encounter *people* in the work-place—made in the image of God, loved by Him, placed by Him in our paths. We can treat them with respect and kindness, or irritation and rudeness. A smile for the grocery checker can do wonders for her aching feet. A "thank-you" to the taxi driver (along with a generous tip) can make his day. Kindness in the face of annoyance can change someone's heart. Simple acknowledgment of a long day or a long line can change someone's outlook.

Sometimes all people need is a smile.

Sometimes all they need is an example.

And that's where we come in. Ready to glow in the dark.

VIEW OF THE KINGDOM OF DARKNESS	VIEW OF THE KINGDOM OF LIGHT
Make a name for myself.	Do all to the glory of God, and not for myself.
God helps those who help themselves.	God helps those who are dependent on Him and take the initiative to trust and obey Him in the power of the Holy Spirit.
Make lots of money for my own pleasure.	Don't lay up treasures on earth, but be a good steward in expanding God's kingdom.
It's a dog-eat-dog world out there, so I must use every method available to succeed.	Do all to the glory of God, and don't yield to expediency.
I use my employees/employer.	I serve my employees/employer.
My job is my most important priority.	Godly character in myself and in my family comes before the job.

ACTION STEPS

Employers...

▶ If you are an employer or have anyone working under your authority, pick one to three people you can compliment this week. Write the compliment in a note, if it seems appropriate, and focus on the job they're doing or an aspect of character that you particularly notice and appreciate.

▶ Spend five minutes in prayer, asking God to examine your attitudes toward your work. Do you "do your work heartily, as for the Lord" (Colossians 3:23)? Do you appreciate that God has you where He wants you and He expects you to "walk in a manner worthy of the calling with which you have been called" (Ephesians 4:1)?

▶ What are ways that you could bring the atmosphere of Christ into your work situation? E.g., initiate/approve a lunchtime Bible study, make sure there are Christian influences in your office Christmas party, sponsor your married employees to a weekend marriage conference to strengthen their relationships.[26]

Employees...

▶ As an employee, working under the authority of another, take a moment this week to compliment your boss or an immediate supervisor for something he/she does that makes the workplace more pleasant or easier to work in.

▶ Spend five minutes in prayer and ask God to show you clearly what your attitude is toward your work. Ask Him for a renewed commitment to "do your work heartily, as for the Lord" (Colossians 3:23). Then, ask Him to point out any way you are not acting with integrity.

▶ Write out a three-point prayer list for your work situation. You could include prayers for your own attitude, for a co-worker who is struggling in some way, for a successful profit margin, for unity, or whatever the Holy Spirit suggests to your heart.

6

Lighting the World

Influencing Your Culture

▶▶ *Carl and Nancy joined the long line of mourners appropriately dressed, waiting to walk slowly by Jackie's casket. They instinctively held hands, warding off the inevitable sense of awkwardness as best they could. Carl searched the crowd for Jackie's husband but couldn't find him. Nancy quickly scanned the crowd to make sure she had worn the right thing to this sad occasion, as if she could do anything about it now. She wondered about Jackie's three grown daughters and what they must be feeling this morning.*

Jackie looked almost normal in the casket. What a strange custom, dressing up and peering at a dead body as if you could make a connection. And how ridiculous for Jackie to die at fifty-four. Unnatural. What a waste. And what in the world would Bob do now, living by himself? Where was the sense in it all?

Separately, but so alike (after all, they'd been married over thirty years), Carl and Nancy allowed themselves a moment to consider their own mortality. This is when it begins, when you see your friends dying. When you recognize that you're the same age, the same build, with similar eating and exercise habits. Carl made a mental note to check with his investment counselor. Nancy made a mental note to remind Carl to check with his investment counselor.

They maneuvered to a seat on a back aisle for a quick getaway should they need one, and sat back to people-watch. Streams of people came through the double doors into the sanctuary—blacks, whites, Asians, Latinos, old, young, so many smiling, embracing each other. Too many smiles. Way too much chatting.

Then in walked Bob and the girls and their husbands, and Carl and Nancy could hear the sniffles all around them. That was more like it. The pastor rose and greeted the crowd. There was music, prayer, a short message on the brevity of life and the life eternal awaiting believers in Jesus Christ, and then came the time for short testimonies about "what Jackie meant to me."

For all Carl and Nancy knew, Jackie was merely a good neighbor, someone whose house you could walk into to borrow an egg if you needed one. She threw parties for the neighborhood on national holidays, volunteered at the nearby elementary school, and occasionally took a temp job if she and Bob wanted to take a more elaborate vacation. There wasn't much of interest you could say about her, they thought.

But one by one a slew of young women stood up to comment on the impact Jackie had made on their lives. They spoke of her availability, of her wise counsel, of her confidentiality. They talked about this legacy she had left in their lives and how it had inspired them to get involved with others.

Carl and Nancy were accustomed to thinking of "legacy" in financial terms. Recently they had been calculating their net worth and discussing what they should leave their two children and what they should spend on retirement. It hadn't occurred to either of them that a legacy could take another form.

They listened intently to the rest of the testimonies about Jackie's influence, and particularly to the parting words by the pastor.

"Jackie wasn't a woman who measured her worth in the world's terms. She didn't have a college degree or make much money. She didn't discover a cure for cancer. But she left a contented husband who knows she loved him, three daughters who are using her life as a role model for their own, and a couple of grandchildren who thought she hung the moon. She also left countless young women whose lives have been changed by her faithful commitment to mentor them. She was their friend, their confidant, and in many cases their mother. So if you're sitting there wondering what purpose there was in Jackie's relatively short life, look around you."

Carl and Nancy did just that.

Discipling the Culture

Ultimately, this is a book about legacy, what we leave in our wake, what kind of impact we make, how we allow God to use us. It's about choosing to live in such a way that lives are different because of our influence.

Thank God! What He works out in us and through us into other people *lasts!* And its fragrant influence spreads like the proverbial ripples on a pond, from one person to a family to the church to the marketplace…and ultimately society is different.

We call this "discipling the culture." It is a process. Whether someone is converted to Coca-Cola or Jesus Christ, they go through a process. James Engel, a noted missiologist, gave his name to it, calling the process Engel's Scale.[27] For the sake of brevity, look at it this way: People move

- from awareness to interest
- from interest to decision
- from decision to commitment
- from commitment to application
- from application to reproduction.

We disciple individuals, affinity groups, and even cultures as we allow the Holy Spirit to use us to help process them along this scale.

The Scriptures present many examples of this process, from the woman at the well (John 4), to the blind man and the Pool of Siloam (John 9), to Nicodemus (John 3), and on and on, even including the disciples, who followed Jesus and in the process believed in Him and obeyed His teaching.

Jesus met people where they were; addressed their needs, questions, and assumptions; and moved them to another level of understanding and commitment to Him. Some embraced Him as Savior right off. Some had to see a miracle or two.

Regardless, all of us, all the New Testament examples and all Christians since then, in one form or another, have gone through some sort of *wooing,* some series of experiences or revelations—some taking moments, some taking years—that make up our journey of faith.

A friend wrote up for us an incident where he sensed he was part of this wooing process:

As I boarded the plane, I was thinking to myself how nice it would be to have an entire row to myself. You know, be able to stretch out, lie down, and get up and use the restroom without having to fight my way to the aisle. So as I sat down next to the window I said a prayer to God for deliverance from the strange people of the world that would try to take the seats next to me.

Moments later, though, as I was staring out into the black abyss pricked with lights, my dreams of sprawling out across the seats in blissful slumber were shattered as a young man about my age came and sat next to me. But rather than sitting there in silence, wallowing in my frustration, I said, "Hi, I'm Sean."

"Jack," he said.

"Nice to meet you," I said with half my heart.

"Same," he replied.

"So, do you live in Atlanta?"

"No, I'm on my way back to Seattle."

And the small talk went on like that when I hit the big red button. "What do you do there?"

"I'm a tattoo artist."

"That's cool...so do you have a girlfriend?"

"No," he said, "I'm gay."

Now, as I am a man who wholeheartedly appreciates the female sex for everything it is and was created to be, I could have completely tuned myself off to this guy and just tried to pass the time as quickly as possible. But instead of reacting how I would naturally to the situation, I decided to do my best to be like Jesus. "Oh," I said...

As we kept talking (and maybe as he saw I didn't run for the hills when he told me he was gay), Jack really began to open up to me. He talked about his family and their lack of support in his sexual preference, his job, his tattoos. It was...real. I told him about what I did and how I was involved at my church and how I had once been sent to a drug and alcohol rehab, but had given my life to Jesus during that time.

I truly felt like I was treating this man the way that our Lord would have. I wasn't preaching at him and showing him all of the Scriptures on hell and damnation and I didn't try to come across as super-righteous or having it all together. I was real. And I could tell that he was totally taken aback by this Christian young man who wasn't judging him, was open about his own shortcomings, and was willing to get to know him.

So by the end of our flight, it wasn't I who invited him to church; he told me that he was interested in coming and checking it out. He said it sounded cool, different than what he had grown to believe about church and the Christians inside of it. I was like, wow! All I had done was my best to show this guy the love that I believed Jesus would have shown to him and I ended up feeling like I sowed seeds that would reap a harvest in this man's life, and bring him into our glorious hope of eternity.

Can you imagine how many bricks came down off what might have been a rather large wall for that young man from Seattle? Can you imagine how he felt about this Christian guy speaking to him face-to-face, even though he knew they didn't agree on lifestyle choices? We all have opportunities to speak to the culture around us and to present the love and forgiveness of Christ. But we have to work at it.

So we come back to the whole idea of the world's spiritual battle, light against darkness, truth against lies, hope against despair. Satan is out to disrupt the discipling process anywhere he can, and we have to fight punch with punch to keep him from winning. That's why we have to take every opportunity we can to penetrate life with truth, hope, and light.

That's the very essence of glowing in the dark.

Why Bother?

Before we address the "how" of this issue, let's look at the "why." Why should we concern ourselves with the culture? Isn't it a lost cause? Do any of us have the energy? Does God really expect us to *do* something?

Why reach the culture? What is our biblical mandate?

God has put us here to glorify Him—that's the be-all and end-all of life. To that end, He's given us three mandates: the Great Commandments (to love Him with all our heart and to love our neighbors as ourselves), the Great Commission (to make, baptize, and teach disciples, i.e. evangelism and discipleship), and what we call the Cultural Mandate (to rule, subdue, and steward the earth).

Way back in the Garden of Eden men and women were charged with responsibility for their environment. It began with the Garden itself and ultimately included all the earth and its inhabitants. (This includes a careful stewardship of natural resources, though we don't have room in this book to cover that concern.)

We are both evangelists by conviction. First and foremost, we want to see people come to Christ. We've seen masses of people make complete turnarounds in their lives as a result of evangelistic meetings, like the one in Korea in 1982 where one million people crowded together on an airstrip in the rain. We've talked to people one-on-one and watched the transforming power of Jesus Christ begin in their eyes. But the culture remains a challenge. Somehow, even with millions of Christians in the world, even with America's Judeo-Christian roots, the purifying power of the Gospel has not prevailed.

We Christians have been comfortable in the backseat for too long, letting secular and anti-Christian religious philosophies set the agenda. In too many cases we have become a harmlessly curious ghetto, a tourist trap that has lost its drawing power, its light, and its salt. Under our watch, despite our convictions, the postmodern philosophy of situational faith, flexible values, and relentless skepticism has become the mind-set of the day.

Yes, we have lost our glimmer and our taste. But we can regain it if we, in the power of the Holy Spirit, will learn to lovingly communicate and helpfully confront the culture with biblical truth, giving people as many opportunities to say yes to Jesus as we can. We must add the covert witness of the body of Christ at large to the overt witness of the Church (from the pulpit, at Billy Graham Crusades, showings of the

Jesus Film, Promise Keepers and Women of Faith rallies, etc.). We can move people closer and closer to the gospel by communicating truth in nonthreatening ways, building warm relationships over a sustained period of time, and providing value-added resources and tools, all with great humility and transparency and without a shred of compromise.

In the process, we saturate our spheres of influence with attitudes that question situational ethics and make God a compelling topic of conversation. This is the job of the body of Christ. This is in part what Jesus meant when He said to Peter that "the gates of hell shall not prevail against [the church]" (Matthew 16:18, KJV).

Progressive Discipleship

Good progressive discipleship gets in the face of the culture by going onto the "secular" turf with truth in a loving, powerful, winsome, practical, and provocative way. Progressive discipleship is characterized by not being just against things, but radically *for* things. The Word of God has the answers to every major problem individuals and cultures face.

My associate and I (Ron) were in San Francisco meeting with the management team of a large company. In the middle of our very first meeting a big, rough guy told us in front of everyone that he wasn't interested in what we had to say. He suspected we might be Christians and he warned us not to "dump your religious stuff" on him. He said his wife was a Christian and that was enough exposure for him.

I couldn't help but reply, "I hope you're not a bigot! Here in San Francisco where you're open to all sorts of lifestyles and philosophies? How about this—you be open to us and we'll be open to you." He had to agree after that argument, and he participated reluctantly every month. One month we dealt with stress, another with conflict resolution.

Several months down the road we talked about viewpoint, how we need to have the right perspective about life and the situations around us in order to be healthy and happy (in actuality, Philippians 4:6–9). Within that discussion I asked the team about their inner lives. We talked about getting centered on truth and about how whatever is at the center of your life is your "god."

A week later that angry man from our first meeting called my associate. "You and Jenson are driving me nuts!" he said. "I keep thinking about what's at the center of my life, and I realized it's me and that's not good! I want you to help me get centered."

"What do you mean?" my associate asked, knowing very well what he meant.

"I want…you know…this…Jesus," he said. "I want Jesus."

He came to Christ, we coached him on his life, and subsequently he sent an e-mail to his team to this effect: "I know I'm a strong person, but I also know I'm weak in setting and following through on right priorities. If there's anything in my life you think I need to change, send me an e-mail. I'll take you out to lunch and we can talk about it. Help me be the best person I can be."

Our friend Bob Buford has written a book called *Halftime* about the unease people feel as they get older and realize they're not making much of a difference in the world. He urges business entrepreneurs to move from success to significance by becoming *social* entrepreneurs, i.e. using their influence to help transform society.

God Must Become the Issue

As our San Francisco executive came to realize, God is the central issue and the answer to the deepest needs of man.

My (Bill) son Brad's book, *God Is the Issue,* makes the point that we have to reframe the questions of our day. He says we will be able to win the culture war only "by making the God of the Bible the central issue within our culture. Debating the issues apart from the larger context of God Himself is the practical equivalent of rearranging the deck chairs on the Titanic while it sinks beneath the waves."[28]

His point is that we waste our energies by debating the issues that concern us from a defensive position. He urges us to reframe the debate and ask: Where is God in this? Much more important than wrestling with political philosophies or individual hot buttons is presenting the Living God, the One True God, the God who loves us, died for us, forgives us, and has an incomparable plan for our lives.

The strength of our message lies in who God is. As Brad writes, "What we believe to be true about God will determine how we live and relate to those around us."[29]

Gino and Pam understand this. They are a perfectly matched couple. Both are short, slim, and attractive. Both are hairdressers and work together in their own business. Both have passionate personalities. And equally passionate tempers. Both have come through hard times, in their marriage and before, and have learned to lean on Jesus, the author and finisher of their faith.

Their mutual struggles have served them well, building their faith in God and in each other. As they continue to see God work in their relationship, they also continue to make a mark in the lives of their clients and employees. Under their nimble fingers sit men and women, young and old, every one a captive audience.

Like all hairdressers before them, Gino and Pam are experts in opening conversations and getting their clients talking. But they have an agenda not all hairdressers have— they want to see minds and hearts and relationships turning to Jesus. They have a disarming way of presenting their own failures and connecting with their clients, and then explaining very clearly just how they benefited from their failures and what place God had in restoring their relationship.

Just recently Gino and Pam hired a new employee going through a difficult divorce that she initiated. Gino has seen God protect and transform his own marriage and is not shy about challenging others to give Him a chance. Day after day he asked his new employee questions about her situation and encouraged her to take another look at things.

Then one afternoon Gino left a hurried "call me ASAP" message on Pam's cell phone. Pam called as soon as she could, and he told her their new hairstylist had decided *not* to go through with her divorce, that she and her husband are reconciling, to their boys'—and Pam and Gino's—great delight.

We love this portrayal because it is such a clear picture of what it means to be salt and light in our culture. Gino and Pam speak about Christ with the same effortless enthusiasm that they speak about their four children. The result is that their clients and employees grow comfortable with making God the issue.

Everyone that Gino and Pam talk to about Christ moves a step closer to a choice about what they will "do" with Him.

And that's progressive discipleship.

So how do *we* go about it?

Be a Model

Like Gino and Pam, our first method of making God the issue is by *modeling* it. Modeling isn't being perfect, but progressing into all God has created us to be. It means we see ourselves through God's eyes—created in His image, loved, fallen, flawed, forgiven, and with unlimited potential. It means we walk daily with the mantle of understanding and grace covering us. We confess our bad attitudes, forgive annoying people, and thank God for both the pleasant and the difficult circumstances that confront us. We speak in kind words and live patiently with the people around us.

In short, we "walk in the Spirit." We keep ourselves in the conscious presence of Christ and allow His Word to fill our thoughts. We do this as we confess our sins to God, experience His forgiveness, yield ourselves unconditionally to his will, and believe the Holy Spirit of God to live in and through us.

Modeling requires we understand what a godly Christian is. Our minds might go readily to what a godly Christian *does*—reading the Bible, praying, and witnessing, all of which are important to making us like Christ. But the bigger question is who a godly Christian *is*.

Jesus, in John 15:7, says, "Abide in Me, and [let] My words abide in you." We can't treat Jesus as a casual friend or the Bible as merely a suggested guidebook for life. "Abiding" in Christ and the Word can be likened to a fish abiding in the sea; it receives all its sustenance and protection from the enveloping ocean. When we model godliness, we live as closely connected to and directed by the Holy Spirit and the Bible as that fish is out in the deep blue. We *are* that fish.

Pollster George Barna, however, says there's almost no distinguishing difference between believers and unbelievers in the area of values. That means too many of us respect Jesus and the Bible, but don't *really* find our sustenance in them. We think we're "abiding" but we go to Jesus only when we're desperate and don't know where to turn. We think we're letting

Jesus' words abide in us, but we tend to use the Bible as a sledgehammer in others' lives, refusing its admonitions and encouragement in our own.

But Christ and His Word are our accountability, our plumb line. They determine and measure our progress as disciples. Sometimes the mirror Scripture and the Holy Spirit hold up to us reveals an image we don't like at all. It's not very pretty. It's not very much like Jesus. But if it weren't for that looking glass, how would believers find out who they really are…and who they have become?

When we abide in Christ, we also convey a sense of freedom, destiny, and familiarity with God to those around us. It's a peace and confidence that simply defies logical explanation. Just think what it means to no longer be bound to the guilt of our sin! Think of the apostle Paul, a highly schooled, deeply religious leader who murdered Christian men and women in the name of God. Can you imagine both the weight of that sin—and then the overwhelming lightness of heart Paul must have felt after encountering Jesus and understanding the truth of forgiveness and salvation? We have that same freedom.

We also have a *purpose* for our lives, a sense of calling so abundantly attractive to the aimless people around us. In the Word we learn that our work matters to God, that there is dignity and value in doing a simple job in the name of Christ. We learn that *how* we work is more important than the *kind* of work God has given us to do. It's all in the mind, and with the right attitude, whatever station we find ourselves in is a place of purpose. Those outside of Christ who observe this in our lives can't help but be curious.

Finally, we walk with God in familiarity, praying easily, conversationally, all day long. We know what He says about Himself so well that we are comfortable with bringing Him into our conversations and relationships. We don't separate ourselves from the world; we engage ourselves, and God, with the world. Just like Pam and Gino.

Take the Initiative

A second way we have an impact on our culture is by *making things happen*. Whoever wins the battle for the lifetime operating system of the culture wins the culture.

Microsoft mogul Bill Gates made billions of dollars with Windows. His success pushed Apple, a great technology in its own right, from a market share of 17 percent down to 3 percent. Why? Because Gates won the battle of operating systems, and an operating system is the "boss" of the computer. All computer software has to submit to that "boss." In the same way, we need to win the operating system for the lives of men and women. Whoever wins the minds of the next generation will win the culture.

We *must* take the initiative. Jesus said, "Go." Why else would He leave us on this unhappy planet after we became children of God?

Our pastor's wife's friend from the previous chapter

joined her local tennis league after her neighbor died. Never again, she vowed, would she be caught unaware of needs at her own doorstep. Christian moms are room mothers and soccer coaches, bringing kindness and absolute values to children and other parents. University students often find themselves in a bastion of liberalism and relativism and should be encouraged to keep making God the issue in the forum around them. Christian men are meeting in Bible studies throughout America and around the world, praying about how to parent their kids or reach their co-workers.

There are countless ways to engage the culture—book clubs, garage sales, voter registration drives, carpools, sports teams, Christmas parties, play groups, supper clubs, Easter egg hunts,[30] vacation Bible school, pool parties, barbecues. Pray and ask God to give you His venue for your witness.

In every sphere there are ways to reshape the operating system of the people we encounter. Every time we connect with people, whether on a large scale or small, if we model Christlike behavior and if we take our stand for values— excellence, honesty, kindness, justice—we have a part in reshaping the culture. As Nike says, "Just do it!"

A longtime staff couple with Campus Crusade made a commitment to change the operating system for some potentially troubled kids in Denver. Colorado UpLIFT was founded in 1982 as a jobs program. At one time fourteen hundred minority high school students were matched with jobs in over two hundred companies. But the leadership discovered that "educational under-achievement and negative work attitudes were tragic realities already blocking their long-term success."[31]

So their vision grew to encompass students all the way down to the upper elementary grades by training the high school kids to mentor the younger ones in the life and attitude skills they would need to become healthy, productive citizens.

Colorado UpLIFT's vision is to "liberate every urban youth held captive." In 2004, over three thousand kids in twenty Denver public schools were involved in the LittleLIFT (elementary school), MiddleLIFT (middle school) and UpLIFT (high school) programs. Ninety percent of UpLIFT kids graduate from high school, as compared to 50 percent of their equally "at-risk" peers. Eighty students received full or partial scholarships at local colleges and universities in 2003.

Why are they so successful? "Longevity and continuity," the leaders say. "We don't give up on kids. *Ever.*"

If anybody has a reason to get involved and not give up on people, it's us! We have the hope within us and the message to share. You who are reading this book also have the conviction to do something about it! How? By being outstanding leaders in your community. By taking the initiative. By not reacting, but being proactive and making things happen.

As Irish philosopher and statesman Edmund Burke said, "The only thing necessary for the triumph of evil is for good men to do nothing." How often have we heard that saying and how often have we nodded and looked around for some *other* good men or women?

Look no further.

Ask God how to take the initiative. Act by faith in Him "who works in you to will and to act according to his good purpose" (Philippians 2:13, NIV).

Take charge in the name of your Savior and King.

If we refuse, if we cower, if we withdraw, our culture will continue its downward plunge. Our presence in society continues to flavor every aspect. Our biblical sense of right and wrong, of decency and indecency, continues to penetrate the darkness—in spite of those who mock us or rage against our stand for Jesus. Who we are makes a difference.

"We are human, but we don't wage war with human plans and methods," Paul says in 2 Corinthians 10. "We use God's mighty weapons, not mere worldly weapons, to knock down the Devil's strongholds. With these weapons we break down every proud argument that keeps people from knowing God. With these weapons we conquer their rebellious ideas, and we teach them to obey Christ" (vv. 3–5, NLT).

We are like a battering ram taking down the walls of a city—not in a rude, obnoxious, offensive way, but in a winsome, loving, dynamic, healthy, thriving, exciting way, bringing truth to the culture, getting people excited about it, and creating a hunger for more.

Identify every area of influence you have. Do you work in an office environment? Outside? Construction? Day care? The food service industry? Are you a teacher, a pastor, a police officer, a flight attendant, a student, a homemaker?

Are you an executive with a burning desire to shape your

professional field? Do you have friends in similar positions itching to make a difference? Can you get together, combine resources and expertise, and change your neighborhood? Can you bring biblical principles into your companies in ways that are accepted by your employees? Can your company start a movement of integrity, a common vision of a healthy, thriving community built around a common good expressed in godly, universal principles? Is there a place where no one else is walking that you can step into and change?

Multiply Yourself

The third thing you can do is *multiply yourself*. We need to celebrate the power of 2 Timothy 2:2: "The things which you have heard from me in the presence of many witnesses, entrust these to faithful men who will be able to teach others also."

There is a reason Jesus ministered to many but focused on a few. He appreciated and demonstrated the principle of multiplication and how it relates to discipleship/coaching. In the long run, more lives and cultures are changed by training a few people how to train a few people, than by one person teaching many but not training them to teach others.

Both of our organizations work within this principle of multiplication, looking for faithful men and women who will build into other faithful men and women.

Isn't "multiplying" the real bottom line? We want to see our society and the world populated by more and more godly, principle-centered husbands and wives, daughters and sons who refuse to compromise in lifestyle and in character, and who care about passing that conviction on to others, particularly those within their own families.

Multiplication doesn't require an advanced degree in theology, psychology, or any other 'ology.' It happens when one person spends concentrated, thoughtful time with another person or small group. It happens between parents and children, grandparents and grandchildren, teachers and students, older and younger friends, man to man and woman to woman. It happens on the professional level and on the friendship level. It's called mentoring, coaching, discipling, even "hanging out together."

Tammy and Sarah are single working women with a love for high school girls and a vision for their spiritual growth. One Friday night a month they take their Bible study of high school girls someplace in the city to serve in some capacity. One night it might be a soup kitchen; one Friday afternoon it could be a home for abused women or pregnant teenagers. They're showing these girls what it means to step out of well-worn comfort zones. Sometimes the steps are actually leaps of faith, but always the landings bring great joy and fulfillment.

Kathy began serving meals to the homeless back when she was a single mom. She had a deep concern both for the unfortunate and to instill a heart of compassion within her own children.

Kathy's daughter, Julia, remembers:

"When Mom was a single parent and we were eating

macaroni and cheese and hot dogs because we couldn't afford anything else, we still gave food to the poor. When we barely had any toys, we would take toys down to the shelter. Mom reminded us constantly that though we didn't have much money, we had more than they did because we had a house and car."

A grandmother in Cincinnati went through our (Ron's) Life Coach Foundation[32] training to become a life coach. As it happened, she found an added benefit that far exceeded her initial expectations. Part of her training certification required her to coach four people...and she had a week's vacation with her four grandchildren (ages six to twelve) coming up.

So she took her materials along and taught her grandkids for a week. Each one took notes and came up with valuable insights for their own situations. The principle on "making things happen" got them talking about how to handle a bully at school. They talked about how they could make better decisions and how to turn negative attitudes into positive ones.

This grandmother has a new operating system that she's been taught to transfer to others. Her grandchildren aren't her only "mission field," but she is so excited that she now has a tool to bolster her relationship with them. She will have a much greater impact on their lives because her investment involves not just grandmotherly contact but character and worldview.[33]

There are hundreds of thousands of grandparents (the average age of a grandparent in America is forty-eight!) shaking their heads over the misdirection of the emerging generation. And there are hundreds of thousands of other seniors with time to kill and a passion for the Lord.

Consider this His call to you! Multiply yourself! Mentor a young parent...or a young teenager. Get *very* involved in your grandchildren's lives, or in the lives of kids whose grandparents aren't around. Coach them in the Word of God. Hold them accountable in the area of their character and attitudes. Show up at their games and concerts. Take them on vision trips to broaden their understanding of the world and to help them put their lives into a big-picture perspective. Invest in young lives, and in that way invest in the future of our nation and the world. Pray for them. Pray with them.

Look for every opportunity to get engaged in any way in society. But realize this: The more you can tie your engagement to helping people think and live biblically, the better. Keep in mind Engel's Scale, and strategize how you can be part of wooing people to faith in Christ every day of your life, in one way or another.

Impact on a National Scale

Before we close this chapter, we want to give you a glimpse of believers who are glowing in the dark in an entirely different landscape in another place in our world.

How does this city-on-a-hill phenomenon impact a nation far away from the shores of North America?

The African nation of Uganda is a far cry from the culture most of us live in, and the obstacles to a healthy society are enormous. But things are happening there that demonstrate the power of God, the impact of prayer, and the influence of many who recognize the powerful spiritual battle.

In the year this book is being written, 2004, the nation of Uganda stands at a critical juncture in her history. Forces are coming together to help this troubled nation continue its move *down* from its designated spot as the second most corrupt country in the world.

It's around this need of battling corruption that the following people have come together.

Kampala Pentecostal Church

"Kampala, downtown, English."

The voice of God was that clear, and the call was that simple. In 1983, after confirmation that this *was* God speaking, Canadians Gary and Marilyn Skinner and their family moved to downtown Kampala, the capital of Uganda, to start an English-speaking church. Kampala Pentecostal Church has since grown into a cell-based community church of twelve thousand people. Emerging from decades of deep spiritual darkness, Kampala is beginning to enjoy an unprecedented spiritual awakening. Lives are glowing in the darkness.

But even in the midst of this joyous spiritual renewal, KPC has watched over 2,000,000 Ugandans die since AIDS spread like a smothering blanket across Africa. With those deaths, 1,100,000 children have been orphaned. The scope of that number (*have you ever tried to count to one million?*) might often discourage people from responding in any kind of concerted effort. God was working, however, giving the Skinners a new compassion for Uganda's orphans.

In 1992, KPC formed Watoto Child Care Ministries. Growing out of this ministry of mercy, Children's Villages have been established. These are groups of homes housing eight children, one housemother, and a housemother-in-training clustered around a school. Currently, over twelve hundred children are being cared for in this holistic home environment, going to school, coming to know and grow in the Lord.

Certainly it would be enough to be about this wonderful work of the Spirit, caring for orphans. But there's more involved. Gary Skinner has a passion to see the transformation of his adopted nation. The church's mandate is "to impart the life of Christ to the people who are leaders in [Uganda]." With his eye for leadership, he is ensuring that the children his church cares for understand that *they are the future leaders of Uganda*. These orphaned children are growing into whole, vital men and women of God who will bless their country and the kingdom of God.[34]

The Women of Harmony

Added to the influence of Kampala Pentecostal Church are the prayers of a Ugandan businesswoman named Olivia and a group of her peers she calls "Harmony." For many years the women of Harmony have been praying for the spiritual and social health of Uganda—from the horrendous days of Idi Amin until the present.

In 1999 Olivia attended an event where the two of us (among others) spoke about living a life honoring to God. In particular, she heard of the Rebuilding the Mental Infrastructure of the Nations[35] project on which our organizations are collaborating.

She began "pestering" me (Ron) to come to Uganda to teach the Proverbs-based life skills necessary to help their country deal with corruption. At great personal sacrifice of time and money, Olivia and Harmony set up events with national leaders and organized seminars for believers *and* unbelievers about building godly principles into the country. And she prayed and prayed and prayed.

Olivia and her colleagues in Harmony continue to work to move this strategy forward. They have mobilized high-ranking leaders in the country. They have set up prayer breakfasts and strategy meetings with top government officials. They have trained and coached the top echelon of the police department, and have now been given the opportunity, along with coaches from Kampala Pentecostal Church, to train all fifteen thousand police officers in Proverbs-based leadership and life skills.

How did all of this happen? Because this one woman had a vision, trusted God to do "exceedingly abundantly beyond all she could think or believe" and selflessly took the initiative to change her world.

From all over Uganda's capital, it's plain to see.

Olivia and the Women of Harmony are glowing in the dark.

VIEW OF THE KINGDOM OF DARKNESS	VIEW OF THE KINGDOM OF LIGHT
Sees spiritual life and faith as limited to personal practice and church settings.	Sees spiritual life and faith as applicable to and penetrating every sphere of life.
Believes God is interested only in the spiritual side of life.	Recognizes that God has intense interest in the culture and in penetrating it for His Kingdom.
Withdraws from cultural issues.	Engages in cultural issues.
Believes biblical principles should not be communicated in the secular, marketplace culture.	Believes that biblical principles must be communicated in the marketplace—winsomely, positively, and practically.
Exhibits a sense of hopelessness for the transformation of the culture.	Has great hope and a positive attitude about what believers and godly principles can do to influence and transform the culture.

ACTION STEPS

▸ If you died right now, how would you be remembered (including the good, bad, and the ugly)? Write down a few thoughts. Try adjectives like kind, angry, loving, distant, etc. And be honest!

▸ Write out the obituary you would like to have written about you if you lived the life you believed God wanted you to live from this point forward.

▸ Ask three family members or friends to describe the kind of impact you've had on them for good or ill. Again, ask for loving honesty here. In light of this, what kind of impact are you having on your world?

▸ What makes you pound the table? In other words, what breaks your heart in your sphere of interest and influence, and what could you do about this that would help change your world like Olivia is changing hers?

7

Fanning the Flame

*How Are You Changing
Your World?*

▸▸Just as God is using Olivia to influence an entire country, so God can and deeply desires to use you to touch your world. "Glowing in the dark" is just a simple metaphor—a common little catchphrase. Even so, it does a good job bringing to mind the picture we want to convey: tiny, seemingly unimpressive glowing embers heat food, warm hands, light ways, dispel darkness. It's been proven time and time again that one person, one company, one family, one church is enough to effect and sustain a radical change out of all proportion to its size. One city on a hill throws back the darkness for many miles.

The apostle Paul was one of the great lights in the darkness of his day. Timothy, his disciple, received some powerful, enduring words of challenge from Paul that are ours to receive as well.

"I have been reminded of your sincere faith," Paul penned to his young friend, "which first lived in your grandmother Lois and in your mother Eunice and, I am persuaded, now lives in you also. For this reason I remind you to fan into flame the gift of God, which is in you through the laying on of my hands. For God did not give us a spirit of timidity, but a spirit of power, of love and of self-discipline" (2 Timothy 1:5–7, NIV).

Paul reminds Timothy of his rich heritage of faith and charges him to fan the gifts God gave him into flame. Don't be afraid, he says, or think you're not old enough or mature enough to make a mark. God has given us everything we need to do what He asks of us.

All these words can be said of us as well. Whether our heritage of faith is one of generations or one of months, we know God wants us to take the gifts He's given us, the faith He's growing in us, and the opportunities He's presenting to us and fan it all into a big, huge bonfire that draws the world to Him.

In the final chapter of 2 Timothy, and in possibly some of his last words to his young disciple, Paul shares a collection of phrases that describe his short but powerful life and ministry and its reward: "I have fought the good fight, I have finished the course, I have kept the faith; in the future there is laid up for me the crown of righteousness…" (4:7–8).

In essence, he gave Timothy and every one of us a template for glowing in the dark.

Fight the Good Fight

Life is a battle, as we've discussed throughout this book. Every day we have a choice to give in to or curse the darkness, or to light some candles. Get out that matchbox and get busy! And please don't take this battle lightly. It is real, it is lethal, and it is all around you every day. So face it head on, letting God transform your thoughts, your life, your family, your church, your professional life, and your world as you allow the Holy Spirit to empower and embolden you and build the Word of God into your life.

Finish the Course

Do you know where you're going? Your job description is clear—to know God (intimately) and to make Him known (everywhere and in every way possible). Wherever God has placed you He can use you, and He will, if you let Him.

Be Faithful

Just as Paul kept the faith, so must you. This doesn't just mean staying true to the Word of God and His will. That's the starting point. It also means not quitting. You *will* fail. Time after time. Just as we have. Management expert Peter Drucker says the greater a man is the more mistakes he will make. Failing doesn't make a failure; failing to learn from your mistakes and not trying again is what makes a failure. So fail often, but fail forward by adjusting and learning and trying again. Just don't quit, don't give up. Keep moving, trusting in the guidance and the power of the Holy Spirit.

Focus on the Future

Paul was satisfied at the end of his life because he knew he had finished the work God placed him on earth to do. Beyond that, he was utterly convinced that God was waiting in eternity to reward him with an "eternal weight of glory" (2 Corinthians 4:17). He knew that his behavior on earth had consequences here and in heaven, and he kept that in mind throughout his life. He intentionally lived in such a way that he was only loosely attached to the things of the world, because he was only passing through.

So keep your priorities in order like Paul did when he said, "we look not at the things which are seen, but at the things which are not seen; for the things which are seen are temporal, but the things which are not seen are eternal" (v. 18). Live for eternity and the joy of those words of greeting from our heavenly Father, "Well done, good and faithful servant."

This poem, one of our personal favorites, is a perspective builder. Time and again it has reminded us about what really counts.

I counted dollars while God counted crosses.
I counted gains while He counted losses.
I counted my worth by things gained in store.
He sized me up by the scars that I bore.
I coveted honors and sought degrees.
He wept as He counted the hours on my knees.
I never knew until one day by the grave,
How vain are the things that we spend life to save.

AUTHOR UNKNOWN

You can do this! You can glow in the dark with the reflected beauty, majesty, and brightness of God's Son. But *will* you? The choice is yours. Eternity and your lasting legacy hang in the balance.

Please pray with us.

Holy Father, we choose You. Please forgive our failures. We ask You to live in us freely. By Your Spirit, by Your Word, we ask You to transform our thinking and to generate anew Your eternal life and light within us. May others be drawn to the glow of our lives; may they see You in us, moment by moment. May You shine through us to encourage the fallen, lift the faint, and give light in the darkness. We ask it in the Name that is above every name, Jesus, our Savior and Lord. Amen.

NOTES

1. A. W. Tozer, "This World: Playground or Battlefield?" from *The Best of A. W. Tozer* (Grand Rapids, MI: Baker, 1978), 84–86.
2. Ibid.
3. Please visit my website, www.discovergod.org.
4. Donald Grey Barnhouse, *The Invisible War* (Grand Rapids, MI: Zondervan, 1965), 83.
5. Quoted by John Powell, *Abortion: The Silent Holocaust* (Allen, TX: Argus Communications, 1981), 30.
6. James W. Sire, *How to Read Slowly* (Downers Grove, IL: InterVarsity, 1978), 15.
7. Richard M. Weaver, *Ideas Have Consequences* (Chicago: University of Chicago, 1948), 121.
8. J. B. Phillips, *Letters to Young Churches* (New York: MacMillan, 1947), xiv.
9. "Inquiry," *USA Today,* 10 October 1984, 11a.
10. Ibid.
11. Dr. Bob Moorehead, "Fellowship of the Unashamed" in *Words Aptly Spoken*, (Redmond, Washington: Overlake Christian Bookstore).
12. Robertson McQuilkin, *A Promise Kept,* (Wheaton, IL: Tyndale House Publishers, Inc., 1998), 22, 32.
13. HomeBuilders is a series of small group Bible studies/discussions that are very effective in helping couples work through issues in their marriages. They are also outstanding tools to use to penetrate neighborhoods. Check out www.familylife.org for further information on this series of studies that will work with believers and unbelievers alike.
14. Randy Pope, *The Prevailing Church* (Chicago: Moody Publishers, 2002).

15. For more information, visit www.christatwork.com.

16. Interview with Bruce Wilkinson (January 28, 1985).

17. Ed Silvoso as quoted in Os Hillman, "Are We on the Verge of a Workplace Transformation?" *International Coalition of Workplace Ministries*. http://www.icwm.net/articles_view.asp?articleid=432 (accessed April 18, 2005).

18. Marc Gunther, "God and Business: The Surprising Quest for Spiritual Renewal in the American Workplace," *Fortune*, July 16, 2001.

19. Visit Os Hillman's www.marketplaceleaders.org for suggestions. *Marketplace Leader's* purpose is to help men and women fulfill their God-given calling in and through their work life.

20. Os Hillman, "Changing the 80/20 Rule in a 9 to 5 Window," *Mission America Coalition*, September 2004. http://community.gospelcom.net/Brix?pageID=13335 (accessed 16 May 2005).

21. Ron's MAXIMIZER principles, through Future Achievement International (www.futureachievement.com), address these Proverbs-based character qualities.

22. See http://corporate.servicemaster.com/overview_history.asp and http://corporate.servicemaster.com/overview_objectives (accessed April 25, 2005).

23. Interview with Chuck Stair (May 17, 1985).

24. "JetBlue: Flying Higher?" *CBSnews.com,* June 18, 2003. www.cbsnews.com/stories/2002/10/16/60II/main525810.shtml (accessed February 9, 2005).

25. Visit www.in-n-out.com.

26. Campus Crusade's FamilyLife hosts weekend marriage conferences around the country and gives group discounts to employers for their employees. Go to www.familylife.com for more information.

27. Paul Hazelden, "The Modified Engel Scale: Working with God in Evangelism." www.hazelden.freeserve.co.uk/pt02/art_pt068_modified_engel.htm (accessed February 9, 2005).

28. Brad Bright, *God Is the Issue* (Peachtree City, GA: NewLife Publications, Campus Crusade for Christ, 2003). This is a particularly valuable book for marketplace Christians who want

to learn how to reframe the questions so that God, not the issue itself, becomes the talking point.

29. Ibid.

30. To learn about Resurrection Eggs, go to http://www.familylife.com/fltoday/flthisweek.asp?id=2801. You can order them at http://www.familylife.com/ 1-800-358-6329/detail.asp?id=6929.

31. "History," *Colorado UpLIFT*. http://www.coloradouplift.org/history/index.php (accessed February 9, 2005).

32. Life Coach Foundation exists to equip parents and grandparents with character-based life coaching skills and tools that will impact and transform the lives of children and youth, enabling them to become productive and principle-centered citizens. More information can be found at www.lifecoachfoundation.org. Also, information on resources for men to *take the lead* in their homes, churches, and ministries is available at www.takingthelead.net.

33. For more information see www.lifecoachfoundation.org. and www.takingthelead.net.

34. Information gathered from www.watoto.com, www.bayou.com/~lou2247/watoto.html, www.biblesociety.org/sr_24/sr24_uganda14.htm, and cap.estevan.sk.ca/Mercury/2002-04-03/watoto.html.

35. This project is marketed and supported by Future Achievement International in cooperation with multiple ministries and organizations around the world. See www.futureachievement.com.